Life Is A
LESSON

To Dear Kenny,
Best Wishes,
with Thank you for your kindness
& Jamie Gavan

LIFE IS A LESSON

Never Give Up Hope

JAMIE GOVANI

AuthorHouse™
1663 Liberty Drive
Bloomington, IN 47403
www.authorhouse.com
Phone: 1-800-839-8640

© 2012 by Jamie Govani. All rights reserved.

No part of this book may be reproduced, stored in a retrieval system, or transmitted by any means without the written permission of the author.

Published by AuthorHouse   10/15/2012

ISBN: 978-1-4772-2697-1 (sc)
ISBN: 978-1-4772-2696-4 (hc)
ISBN: 978-1-4772-2698-8 (e)

Any people depicted in stock imagery provided by Thinkstock are models, and such images are being used for illustrative purposes only.
Certain stock imagery © Thinkstock.

This book is printed on acid-free paper.

Because of the dynamic nature of the Internet, any web addresses or links contained in this book may have changed since publication and may no longer be valid. The views expressed in this work are solely those of the author and do not necessarily reflect the views of the publisher, and the publisher hereby disclaims any responsibility for them.

THIS BOOK IS DEDICATED TO MY DEAR LATE FATHER, MOTHER, MY GRANDMOTHER, BAA AND ALL MY DEAR GRANDPARENTS.

Mr Amir and Mrs Roshan Karsan
[MUM AND DAD]

CONTENTS

Preface ix
Prologue xiii

Chapter 1 1
Chapter 2   The Full Horror Unfolds 9
Chapter 3   The Great Escape 15
Chapter 4   A New Country, and the Start of Our New Lives 20
Chapter 5   England 25
Chapter 6   Agreement 29
Chapter 7   New Foundations, More Moves 32
Chapter 8   Family Moves 36
Chapter 9   My Year in India 42
Chapter 10   Babies and Business 51
Chapter 11   My Lady of Destiny 65
Chapter 12   Good-bye, Dad. We All Loved You,
             Our Pilot, So Much 69
Chapter 13   Once More, a Life-Changing Turn of Events 75
Chapter 14   Amir's Magnificent Surprise for Me 79
Chapter 15   Bridging That Forty-Year Gap 82
Chapter 16   A Tribute to My Parents and Uncles 96
Chapter 17   . . . And to My Grandparents 101
Chapter 18   Canada Calling 105
Chapter 19   Lincolns 109
Chapter 20   Another Family's Story 112
Chapter 21   My Dear Sister's Tragic Battle 119
Chapter 22   . . . And Not Forgetting the Govanis 125
Chapter 23   Life Is a Lesson 133
Chapter 24   Review and Reflections 135

PREFACE

My memories of one of the most momentous events in the history of mankind are as vivid and as moving today as they were forty years ago. To put them into words, to be handed down from generation to generation, is an ambition I have nurtured for the greater part of my life. Now that my opportunity has finally come, I feel genuinely privileged to have written this book. My life and that of my family was in turmoil, and this ordeal has left many scars on us, but we were just grateful to be alive, because so many innocent people lost their lives through no fault of their own. I have always believed that life is a lesson in itself; sometimes we are faced with such sorrows, but amongst that we must find a little happiness and be able to accept it with open arms, whatever it throws back at us.

Time, of course, has been the enemy. It is only recently that I have found more of it at my disposal, albeit partly for unwelcome reasons. Most of my life, it seems, has been spent working very hard—all hours God sends, as they say. I have raised three children and, as with every mother, the search for any spare time has often seemed more akin to looking for needles in a haystack.

However, in 2010 my world was turned upside down when I was diagnosed with colon cancer. I had major surgery and subsequently spent time—lots of it—just lying in bed. I had a lot of love and help from friends and family, but being a very independent person, I needed to come to terms with the surgery I had gone through. I wanted to manage the best I could, which to a degree gave me a lot of strength. I found myself with lots of time on my hands for the first time, and having so much space on my own brought me a new of tranquillity.

That was an utterly alien experience for me, but I turned it to my advantage by doing some serious thinking. As best I could, I gathered my thoughts about my memories of Uganda that had been embedded in my heart since childhood. I identified two goals: to return to my native Uganda and to write a book about my own experiences there and the life that resulted from my expulsion from that beautiful country. Many times in my life, I have thought of my life and my childhood there, but with time the scars have faded away. Feelings of sadness overtook me sometimes when I thought of my grandparents, economic migrants from Gujarat, India, and their struggles to have to start a new life in Uganda.

Then came the opportunity to realise the first of those goals. There was a very special event coming up in Uganda. It was something very dear to my heart, something of which I was truly very privileged to be a part of and I desperately wanted to go, but it would not exactly be easy because my twins were in the midst of their AS-level examinations. Despite my passionate desire to return to Uganda, I did not want their studies to be disturbed in any way.

Then it happened—a big surprise from my husband, Amir. Without my knowledge, he made the arrangements for a trip that would take the pair of us to Uganda—and we were to leave in a couple of days!

I wondered what Uganda would be like now. As a child, I knew it as the most gorgeous country. I was in love with its delightful greenery, its fertile soil, the hills, the beautiful weather, and above all the wonderful people. When I left, I was only ten years old, merely a child with a free spirit. All this was "mine"—until President Idi Amin took centre stage and destroyed everything. I lived in a beautiful little town where I woke up to the birds chirping around me, and the view of the Kigulia Hills from my window. My family, and many thousands others like us, were brutally expelled from Uganda.

My story now not only recalls that ghastly phase of our lives but also tells of how we settled in Britain and adapted to a totally new way of life, having arrived with little more by way of possessions than the clothes we wore.

I have also taken this opportunity to trace and outline how, long before Amin made his historic mark, those first Asians came to Uganda under colonial rule to build the railway. This book charts the near half-century from my early childhood up to the present day, where

I now have a niece who is half German and other nieces and nephews who are half English. It tells the story of how my family became refugees overnight and lost everything—not only their possessions but also their sense of direction. It recalls the hardships they endured, along with the unity amongst their families and friends that ultimately pulled them through the crisis. A day never goes by that I don't wake up thanking God for keeping us safe.

Not everyone lived to tell the tale. As this book also points out, thousands of innocent indigenous Ugandan people were slaughtered by Idi Amin's army. Colonial rule had divided the country into tribal zones, creating a heightened awareness of individual identity amongst the tribes and their races. Amin took advantage of this and ordered the slaughter of thousands of Ugandans who belonged to various tribes. Hundreds of poor children became orphans and homeless.

As I walked through the streets of Kampala, Uganda's capital, during my long-awaited return to that country, I could see a very different Uganda, one of which I had dreamt—where everybody lived harmoniously in mixed communities, working and playing together. Isn't this what our children want to see today, so that they can live happily side by side, wherever they are?

Accompanying those thoughts floated the great John Lennon song, Imagine, and in particular these words:

> *Imagine no possessions*
> *I wonder if you can*
> *No need for greed or hunger*
> *A brotherhood of man*
> *Imagine all the people sharing all the world*

From the depths of my heart I wanted to salute the Ugandans who, through their kindness, welcomed the Asians to live amongst them for many years. Today, I am also very proud to be a part of a country such as England, which has embraced pluralism, and has enabled my children to grow up in country of great freedom and security. England has a constitutional monarchy. The Queen is a remarkable lady who recently celebrated her Diamond Jubilee.

While writing this book, I revisited my native Uganda and experienced a maelstrom of memories and emotions. We suffered but overcame; so perhaps this book can inspire those that have experienced a similar fate, in one way or another, and a seed of hope would be planted in their hearts.

"Difficulties are opportunities to better things; they are stepping stones to greater experiences. This is only a temporary setback in a particular direction, because when one door closes, another one always opens."

Finally, whilst writing this, I remembered thoughts and images of the most important people in my life, in particular those for whom I feel incredible fondness and for whose unfailing help, support, advice, encouragement and purest love I will be eternally grateful. Without their sacrifices, this would not have been possible.

Prologue

The moment I dreamed of for almost forty years was just minutes away. As I looked out of the aeroplane window that clear, moonlit evening in July 2011, I could see my dream slowly turning into reality. Like a vast carpet of dazzling dots and streaky lines, Kampala, the capital of Uganda and the country's largest city, was gradually spreading itself out beneath me. It was just twenty or so more miles to go before we landed at Entebbe Airport, on the city's outskirts. I was so anxious, nervous and emotional. I kept pinching myself—could this really be happening at long last, or was it all just a dream still? A cruel dream, maybe, to add to the nightmare of my experience back in 1972, when we fled our native Uganda in those darkest days of Idi Amin's brutal, despotic regime.

Idi Amin, the Butcher of Uganda as he became known, was possibly one of the most notorious of all Africa's post-independence dictators, the other being Jean-Bedel Bokassa, Emperor of the Central African Republic. Along with tens of thousands of other Ugandan Asians, we had had our lives transformed almost overnight; we were subjected to scarcely imaginable upheaval and fright as a result of his tyranny. Unlike so many others, we at least still had our lives—but I had never returned to Uganda, until now.

There were about a hundred passengers on that Kenya Airways flight approaching Entebbe International Airport. The stewardesses, in their beautiful African dresses, had offered me food, but I couldn't manage to eat anything. I was just so tense and tearful.

As we descended towards the runway, I said aloud, "Oh my God, am I really doing this after all these years?" I was just ten years old when Amin forced me to flee my country. Now, sobbing for all I was worth as my magic moment came closer and closer, I could sense my fellow passengers looking at me and thinking, "What's wrong with this woman? Has she had a row with her husband?"

They need not have worried; indeed, they could not have been more wrong. Amir, my husband, gave me a firm hug as the plane touched down. Amir was the cause of my tears, yes, but only because he had made this trip of a lifetime possible. After what seemed an eternity, but which was a mere two or three minutes, the steps opened out of the side of the plane and down onto the tarmac. We were in the centre of the plane, and it felt like everybody made their way off at a snail's pace. Amir and I walked down the steps together. We reached the bottom and at that point I was oblivious to everyone, even to Amir. While Amir clutched my hand luggage, I could not stop myself from going down on my hands and knees and kissing and my native land. I was breathing my native air again.

Some of the other passengers feared I had fallen. Several stopped and made to help me up, inquiring, "Are you all right?"

"Oh yes," I replied. "There's no need to worry, I really am okay. Believe me, I am incredibly happy right now." I was back home at last.

Idi Amin was a military leader and President of Uganda from 1971 to 1979. In 1946, he had joined the British colonial regiment, the King's African Rifles, and eventually became a general in the Ugandan army. Dr Milton Obote, the Ugandan president at that time, who was from the Langi tribe, was planning to arrest Amin for misappropriating army funds. This caused a huge rift between Obote and Amin, resulting in a military coup. Amin seizing power while Obote was out of the country at the heads of Commonwealth conference in Singapore.

Amin, now a self-appointed Field Marshall, ordered his troops to seal off Entebbe International Airport. His troops seized Kampala and Amin then proclaimed himself President of Uganda, Commander in Chief of the armed forces, Army Chief of Staff, and Chief of Air Staff. He disbanded the General Service, the intelligence agency, and created the State Research Bureau (S.R.B), based in Nakasero, Kampala, which became notorious as the scene of torture and executions. Hundreds of Langi soldiers that belong to Obote's tribe were massacred and thousands of other civilians were also killed. This torture was a common feature throughout Amin's eight-year reign.

At that time, Uganda was home to approximately 80,000 Asians who were of Indian origin—many had been born in Uganda and were Ugandan citizens. The early Asian settlers had come to Uganda with very little and had worked extremely hard eventually forming the backbone of the Ugandan economy.

On August 4th, 1972, Amin declared that he had had a dream in which God appeared to him and told him that the Asians were crippling his country. This cleansing started with 60,000 Asians being exiled, which was later amended to include all 80,000 of the Ugandan Asian community. He seized businesses and personal properties belonging to the Asians, which were then handed over to his supporters. The Asians were removed from the country with next to nothing, and hundreds of lives were irreversibly changed overnight!

Chapter 1

It has s been many years since I first came to England and I feel very privileged to be part of the British community, which welcomed and accepted me, and my family, in our time of great need. We were faced with a lot of difficulties, such as the language barrier and the harsh British winters, which is something we were not accustomed to. We suffered from poverty and many other hardships as well, but with God's grace we persevered through. Thereafter we were known as the Ugandan Asians.

Prince Saddrudin Aga Khan, then <u>United Nations High Commissioner for Refugees</u>, played a major role in finding a safe haven for those ex-Ugandan Asian citizens who had become stateless. He facilitated the evacuation of displaced people, including my father, two uncles and an aunt, to refugee camps in Europe, with subsequent resettlement of the remainder of the refugees (some had already migrated to countries such as Canada) in some European countries. On a number of occasions, he visited the refugee camps and advised refugees that despite many challenges ahead, they should be strong enough to face them. Language was the first barrier, but one should become bilingual in order to combat this. He also stated that whichever country they would resettle in, they should become a part of it and contribute towards its economy and society in whatever way possible. My father was given an opportunity to make a speech, in which he thanked the Prince and the Austrian government for saving us from Amin's torture.

I hope to demonstrate this pride with this book. What follows is the true story of how this family experienced a nightmare of truly epic proportions, yet still managed to re-establish themselves after momentous upheaval. Throughout the ordeal, they had faith in the ultimate and never lost their belief that by remaining true to themselves, not forgetting their roots, and remaining united, they would pull through hard times.

This is the story of how my family responded to one of the darkest chapters in mankind's history, which simply cannot be left untold. I hope you will be as inspired by it as much as I have been proud to have been a part of it.

I was brought up by my parents, Amir and Roshan Karsan. I was one of six children, with four sisters and a brother, born to God-fearing parents who were extremely kind and whose belief in the righteous path was absolute. My mother is a great blessing to us, someone with great wisdom, energy and tremendous generosity. God has granted me many things in life for which I am very grateful, but without a doubt the best gift he could have given me is the blessing of such kind parents. I would say that my closest friend was my father. He died of cancer six years ago, but we shared such special moments and those will always remain with me.

He was the kind of person who was generous with his advice; he was a happy, respectable and selfless man, who spoilt us, not with gifts but with quality time that he spent with us. I remember when I got back from my first Saturday job, I would spend all the money I earned on clothes and cosmetics, and he would advise me to save a little just to prepare myself for the future. He always advised me that one should not spend a penny more than one's earnings, learning to live within one's means. The present economic recession proves the point.

Dad always taught us that it was better to give than to take, and that friendship should be built on getting close to people without ulterior motives, never expecting anything in return. He prepared us for the days when he would be gone, so we could cope with life, although when the moment arrived, it was very hard for us, especially for my mother. In his absence we often sit together and reflect on what he taught us. During my hospital visits, when I was low, he would come to my mind and remind me to never give up and to accept life with open arms.

Thus this strength of unity and help from the Almighty was what got us through my family's immense suffering. We not only survived, but we also managed to re-establish ourselves after momentous upheaval. Throughout, we understood that life was full of ups and downs and that we should not, could not, ever give up. We never lost faith. We remained true to ourselves, remembering our roots and remaining united.

My mother was just sixteen and my father eighteen when they got married. That seems very young now for marriage, but it was nothing unusual then. My grandfather on my mum's side, Esmail Tejani, was a teacher who was brought to Uganda by the British to teach. With all the hard work that he put into teaching, he was promoted to head teacher at the Masindi Public School. My mother met my father through my grandfather. My father always used to tease her. My mother had long hair and beautiful, large, dark eyes, so he would joke with my grandfather and say she had headlight eyes that scared anyone off from wanting to marry her. So what happened? He had secretly fallen in love with her and ended up marrying her! Throughout our lives, we teased Mum and Dad about this—and each time Dad would just smile.

My siblings and I had a very happy childhood. My early years were spent in Masindi Port, a beautiful village built on Lake Kyoga. It had twelve Asian occupied houses, but all the residents lived like one big family with great support and love for each other, in good times and bad. There was so much love amongst all the residents that if needs be, one would even give up their day's earnings for the well-being of another—and it would be done without any questions. Our household consisted of my dear Grandfather, Kaka, and my grandma, known as Baa; my lovely Uncle Sherali; Mum and Dad; my brother, Ferride; and my sisters, Shaida, Sahera, Shamira, and Naffilla. Uncle Hadi, Uncle Akbar, my twin uncles Hassan and Hussein, Aunt Laila, and Aunt NoorJehaan, known as Begum, were studying or working away from home. My other aunts were Roshan, Gulshan, and Seru bai—father was the eldest. Uncle Sherali was very bright and could have done really well at university, but there were not enough money to educate everyone, and so he sacrificed this potential opportunity to facilitate the education of the rest of the family. He worked very hard for the family without expecting anything in return; his sacrifice was immense.

Masindi Port had a Jamat Khanna, a prayer house, where worshippers would gather every evening. Faith was very important to us, as it is today, and we always believed that success was in the hands of God.

The Asian residents and their families of MasindiPort were:

Lakha Mohamed	Jamatkhana(prayer house)
Popat Karsan	Kara Jetha
Shivji Karsan	Abdul Jamal
Hussein Adam	Abdul Karim
Akbar Mandan	Jamal Jetha
Ebrahim Nanji	Virji Mandan

There was also the Darbar family; Mr Darbar was a local bus driver, a very kind gentleman with generous qualities. Also there were Arsi bhai and his dear family whom the whole village was very fond of.

None of the properties in Masindi Port had an electricity supply or running water; but two properties used generator-backed power and the other houses used lanterns in the night. Water had to be fetched from a well and some was stored in large tanks. It was a tremendous amount of hard work, but the villagers were used to it and never complained.

The buckets would be filled up and carried home, and then the water would be boiled and stored in clay pots, ready to drink. The non-boiled water would be used for household chores. Not having power or water was not a big issue, because we were used to this way of life. If one has never had something in the first place, then one doesn't miss it! If one family were in difficulty, the others would be sure to come and help. There were no cars or other motor vehicles, except for a truck and a Mercedes Benz car owned by Jetha brothers. So occasionally, if an outsider visited in a motor vehicle, all the children would gather around it in awe. It's difficult to imagine now, I know, but back then a car in Masindi Port was a source of great fascination to us. What a contrast to today's world, where cars are in abundance even when they cause so much pollution. I can say one thing, the village was totally free of pollution, and everything was natural.

I remember a great many fruit trees—mangoes, guavas, pomegranate and bananas. The mango trees grew in abundance in the yards of the houses, and there were many other fruit trees in the gardens. My grandfather would pick fruit every day, cutting it into pieces and feeding us all with it without taking a bite first. His love for us was priceless. I remember how there was a swing on the veranda. When

I was a baby, and while my mum and grandma were busy with house chores, my grandfather would put me in that swing until I fell asleep. Even when his hands were tired of rocking the swing, he would make sure I was comforted before he would stop. How lucky was I? We used to own a little pet monkey, which I was very fond of and who was very clever.

The houses in Masindi Port were made of corrugated iron sheets, which kept the houses cool when the weather was incredibly hot. We had a rainy season, but even then the temperatures were always high. I remember that when it used to rain, my mother and grandmother would run out with large drums to fill them up with water in order to save them the hard work of fetching the water from the lake or well. These two women had incredible strength. Food was cooked on something called a sigili, which is a Swahili word for an oven. The sigili was made out of either metal or mud, and the food cooked on it tasted fabulous. White clothes were boiled in them to restore their whiteness. There were no ready-made nappies, so they had to use cloth nappies, which took a long time to wash.

My grandfather, my father, and Uncle Sherali ran a little general store and a sub-post office. My grandfather made mosquito nets and helped in the shop. I sometimes used to see him late at night sewing under a lantern. He was a man of integrity and always true to his word, so if he had promised anyone that the garment would be ready by the morning, he always made sure that it was. There was no electric power, so he had to use a manual sewing machine, which required a lot of energy, but we would never hear him complain. Grandad would go around the nets twice so that they would not tear easily. This way, his customers would have greatly extended the value from the nets.

Grandmother and Mum took care of the household chores and family needs. These two women were strong, not just physically but mentally. There were days when money would be scarce, and this would put a severe strain on the food budget, but for all that, there was always food for the family. We always sat on a mat and shared the food. Baa and Mum would make do with the leftovers or a slice of bread with pickle—but we would never find out that they had not eaten properly. There were hard times, but we were always shielded from them. During the cold nights, the family would light a big bonfire in the open air, and the whole village would sit around it together, cooking and eating cassava, without any worry about the outside world that seemed a million miles away. What one didn't know about, one needn't worry about; such was the innocence. I was concerned with more immediate problems such as chasing butterflies, even though I had no shoes. I actually loved the comfort of not wearing shoes. My best memories were of getting soaked in the rain on a hot day. As soon as it would begin to rain, I would run out just to get soaked and then admire the rainbow, which would glaze the sky after the rain had stopped.

Occasionally, the village would hire a projector to watch Bollywood films in the grounds of the Jamat Khanna, with the whole village sitting down on mats in the evening after finishing their work. We would have plenty of popcorn and other goodies. Sometimes the entire village would picnic on Lake Kyoga, with each household contributing something to eat or drink. The views were incredible: the clear blue skies, the hills and, above all, the tranquillity.

The village lived as a united, single entity. That might be rather difficult for younger people today to understand, but those Asians from Uganda who have since grown up in Britain and elsewhere have never lost that connection with each other. We strongly believe that the seeds of love planted by our grandparents still exist today amongst these families. In fact a couple of years ago I had a reunion.

Masindi Port had a small school, Masindi Port Common School, a police station and a factory (where cotton from sisal and jagri were made), but had no hospital. If straight forward medical care was required, there was a lovely lady called Hawa Masi who was very good with ayurvedic medicines. However, for other cases one had to go to the Masindi Hospital, which was forty-six kilometres away. Once, Uncle Akbar fell from a swing at school and suffered severe head injuries; he had an open wound and blood poured down his face, so he was rushed off to that hospital to be stitched up, with my grandma in tears as she watched him go.

My father would travel to Kampala on Jamal Jetha's trucks to buy fabrics for the retail outlet. These trucks were not like what we have today. There was no power-steering, the roads were muddy and full of dust and potholes. We still see these roads in poor parts of the world today, and people still learn to cope with them—just as we did in our day.

When I was about nine years old, some of the family moved to Masindi, a town where there were better business prospects and schools. Uncle Sherali, Grandpa, and Grandma stayed behind.

Dad and Uncle Hadi bought a building that comprised a shop and a public bar. Uncle Hadi would have done very well at school and beyond, but he had to give up on that idea because of the lack of funds. Instead, he had to put his head down and work, in order to support the family. Both the brothers, together with Ramde Ram, worked very hard to build the partnership business. Ramde Ram was a very kind soul. He returned to India some years prior to the Asian expulsion, where a distant relative murdered him. The remainder of the family now live in Leicester.

Following Uncle Hadi's marriage, we were two families living behind the shop. All the children went to Masindi Public School. My grandfather, Tejani, was a very devoted head teacher there in 1953, well before I was born. I was not aware of this because he had passed away when I was a toddler, but on my visit back to Uganda, a teacher at the school dug out his name from one of the books about the history of Masindi Public School. What an amazing surprise!

My father built a good reputation in Masindi and was well liked by the locals. His fair-minded nature and kindness to his fellow beings earned him the nickname, Rafiki, which in Swahili means friend. If anyone needed help, no matter what religion, colour, or status, he only had to knock on our door. Dad would help with filling in forms for planning. He was self-taught and could speak many Ugandan languages such as Munyoro, and Langi, as well as English.

Not surprisingly, he became involved in politics. Dad was a Town Councillor.

My father tried many projects to make money for the family. Dad had to find fresh revenue streams to fund increasing household expenses and school fees. He also became an agent for Daihatsu and Hino vehicles in Masindi, representing Ramzan Motors, based in Kampala. He was very good at this, and the return was good. In the three years prior to our departure in 1972, Dad had sold over a hundred vehicles for Ramzan Motors in the Bunyoro district. Dad and Ramzan Madhani became great friends. One of Dad's qualities was his honesty, which served to increase his repeat business.

My mother told us—and we still laugh at this today—of an incident where my father "had the devil in him" and tried entering the fishing industry, despite having no prior knowledge of it! He decided, following advice from a relative, to go to the fishing port of Butiaba, where he filled his Opel estate van (USL 48) with fish to sell at Kampala fish market, some two hundred and forty kilometers away. Unfortunately, with the high temperature, the fish rapidly spoilt. He had put so much hard work into this venture, and it turned into a minor disaster. He was so disappointed and angry with himself. It took a long time for the smell in the van to disappear. This seems funny to us now, but when it happened, knowing my Dad, he must have felt so bad and angry with himself for letting us down. If only I could turn the clock back and give him a great big hug for trying so hard. He deserved it!

At this stage in my life, after having my own children, I understand how hard it must have been for him, keeping up with the family's demands. Knowing my father, he must been so disappointed with this unsuccessful venture, because he would interpret it as being a failure. But in our eyes, he did his best.

Chapter 2

The Full Horror Unfolds

The date that was to change history and transform the lives of tens of thousands of Ugandan Asians was Saturday, August 5, 1972. Stunned, in its absolute, literal sense, is the only word to describe how we all felt at that moment. It was eight o'clock in the evening. We had no television set, but my father always listened to the BBC World Service.

I was ten years old and had grown up in this pleasant country without a care in the world. My brother and sisters would play in the woods, and if they fell or otherwise hurt themselves, my grandmother would call out and ask for haldi (turmeric) to put on their wounds. There was such comfort in being nursed by Grandmother rather than a doctor; only in extreme cases would the doctor be called out. Until that historic date in 1972, this was the limit of my concept of pain. Not even in my wildest dreams had I ever come close to conjuring up a scenario involving the changing of my world overnight with expulsion from the country where I was born, and which I loved with all my heart and soul. But that was precisely what happened. I was young, yes, but not so young that I could not understand what was going on, once the shock had sunk in. As we sat around the radio to listen to that auspicious news bulletin, no one could mistake the gravity of what we were hearing. Indeed, the statement was so awesome, so frightening, that those who heard it struggled to believe it at first.

Idi Amin's voice came over the airwaves solemnly announcing that all the Asians in Uganda must leave the country. He clearly stated,

"The Ugandan Asians must leave." At first, people thought it must be some sort of a joke. We thought that this was just some sort of threat made in order to gain popularity with the indigenous population, who also had no idea what this man was doing. There were rumours floating around that Idi Amin felt rejected when Mrs Jayant Madhvani, a rich Asian widow, had turned down his advances causing him to retaliate by attacking all Asians.

But it was all real enough, as we were soon to discover. Explaining his decision, Amin said that Asians had been brought to Uganda by the British to build the country's railway. This work was now complete, Amin explained, and so the Asians were no longer required in Uganda. He declared they must leave—simple as that. For good measure, he added the bizarre comment that the Asians had "milked the economy" and had never given anything back. Ironically, the Asians had been amongst those seen dancing in the streets when, just a few months earlier, when Amin had come to power following the overthrow of the Obote government. Now this man was kicking them in the teeth.

It was true that the initial Asian migration had come to East Africa to build the railway under the British, when India had been a British colony, but it was also true that these people worked extremely hard in all fields. Some were labourers and some were clerks and traders, supplying goods to the local population. India was one of Great Britain's biggest colonies, the Jewel in the Crown of the Empire. In many ways the Asians became a part of the fabric of Uganda. They created wealth, making positive and significant contributions to the country's economy, and the more adventurous entrepreneurs built factories. People were reluctant to take Amin's announcement seriously. At first they could not believe that anyone would be so silly as to expel Asians who were in control of a significant part of the economy. But the seriousness of the situation and the truth dawned on us soon enough.

In a radio broadcast that was reproduced on the front pages of all the newspapers the next morning, Amin confirmed the expulsion of Asians holding British passports; similar broadcasts followed in quick succession. A few weeks later, he announced that all non-citizen Asians—meaning all those holding Kenyan and Tanzanian passports—also had to leave. Then he fooled the educated Asians, the professionals, into believing that they could stay because they were good for the economy. But in the final analysis he stated, unequivocally and unmistakably, that all Asians must leave Uganda.

He made no effort to hide his hatred for the Asians. Verification of Uganda citizenship was carried out by spot checks on Asians who were required to carry identity cards, known as Kipande. People would queue for hours to claim Identity Cards only to be humiliated by being told in some cases that there was not sufficient evidence to formally declare that they were Ugandan citizens, and so they could not be granted those rights. This meant that people like my father, who were born in Uganda, were made stateless overnight. This happened to hundreds of people, and they all became refugees.

Every day, after that first, unforgettable news bulletin, there would be a new announcement, a new law passed to make it harder for the people to claim their right to stay in Uganda. Things became more and more difficult and the tension and fear grew. There was no way to protect one's assets; the government monitored every transaction. Even airlines ticket had to be endorsed by the Bank of Uganda. You couldn't even take your car out of the country. Amin made sure all the Asian assets in the country were monitored very closely, so that they would not be able to take anything with them when they left, except the £50.00 that each family member was allowed to take out of the country.

He was very clever at creating a situation where it would be impossible for any businessman to get out of Uganda with anything worthwhile. This harassment was kept up mercilessly and ruthlessly, with many arrests that appeared to be solely to frighten the rest if the community and warn them of the consequences of disobeying his government.

There was total chaos. Amin's army seized every opportunity to take whatever they set their eyes on, and this harassment spread throughout Uganda. New, untrained recruits quickly indulged in atrocities of their own to satisfy their greed. Many wealthy people were beaten, and some even murdered—typically by being tied up, suffocated and then thrown into the boots of their cars. The cars would then be pushed into the bushes, never to be found. Sometimes the bodies would also be thrown into the bushes and left to rot. A person might be driving along when he would suddenly be stopped by armed soldiers and then thrown out of his vehicle, which would promptly be stolen by the soldiers. In some cases, victims would be beaten up and left for dead near the roadside, while others were taken away and locked up for months. In the worst cases, detainees were never seen again.

The streets in the evenings were completely empty, people were simply too frightened to go out. There was a truly ghostly feel about the streets. I remember going with my aunt to be buy a few household necessities from the market, and on my way back we saw a great big army truck coming towards the market. My aunt grabbed me and pulled me behind a parked car. If we had not hidden from the army, they would have searched us, with consequences one dare not imagine.

There were long queues outside the British High Commission in Kampala, with people sleeping outside without food or shelter. These people wanted to get out of Uganda no matter the cost, to save their families and themselves from torture—or worse. In particular, people were frightened for their young daughters as many teenagers were captured and raped. My father did not take Amin's historic announcement seriously at first. He was born in Uganda and had always treated the locals well—he called himself Ugandan. Eventually, the Asians began to recognise the stark reality as Amin's words sank in and the horrific sequence of events unfolded. People were upset, shocked, and depressed, and they turned to each other for help with a growing sense of community spirit. Amin's reign increasingly became one of sheer terror.

The deadline for the expulsion was November 8, 1972, and we were left in no doubt that he meant it. The British High Commission worked long hours to accommodate the Asians preparing to leave. There was a time when the British High Commission was only open for half a day, five days a week; while the Uganda High Commission was open all hours. But Amin was a man in a hurry, and he became impatient. On one occasion, he ordered his army to arrest a hundred British citizens and put them in jail. At this point, the British High Commission hired more people and began to open for longer hours, to assist with the expulsion process.

Amin censored the press, ensuring a steady stream of headlines on the front pages of the newspapers that were expressly designed to scare the Asians. He certainly succeeded in putting fear into these people, so much so that they actually feared for their lives and were driven to depart prematurely. In many cases they left behind all their possessions—their homes, their businesses and their cars. This was exactly what the ruthless dictator wanted. It was like some sort of weird game to him, he toyed with everyone.

His army was given all the authority they needed to steal, beat, rape, and even kill. Sadly, it seemed they were in their element. Many of these soldiers were not properly trained; they had joined the army through greed and proved to be totally undisciplined. As one early and tragic example, the first contingent of Asians that left Uganda, en route for India, were on their way to Mombasa to join their ship when they were stopped, searched and beaten. Then they were lined up on the ground, face down, and the women were raped. I remember my aunt telling me how the peace of one evening in Kampala had been shattered when the army knocked on her door. My uncle opened it and was confronted by five soldiers. In their native language, they demanded, "Where is the money hidden?" My uncle said there was no money in the house, whereupon they beat him. When my aunt heard the noise from the garden, she told the children to hide while she ran in to try to deter the attackers. At this point, they were spraying the mattresses with a machine gun to see if any hidden money would be revealed. They found nothing, so they resorted to kicking my aunt onto the ground. Mercifully, one of the soldiers still had a little humanity about him, he asked his colleagues to leave the house because there was clearly nothing there to steal and he persuaded them to stop kicking my aunt.

People were robbed of their cash in broad daylight. Some would have their faces stomped on by the boots of the soldiers. Law and order appeared to have broken down completely. Amin had warned that the punishment for not leaving the country would be jail and torture. My grandmother, a British Protectorate passport holder, with her twin sons and daughter decided that for their safety they should leave immediately for England.

Amin had quickly established his reputation as a despot, and his army had become notorious. They killed large numbers of the Langi people, who belonged to Obote's tribe. On one occasion, his army arrested my Uncle Sherali because he refused to open the sub-post office outside opening hours. They took him and had him locked up. Generally, anyone who was arrested and locked up would never be seen again, but my uncle was one of the lucky ones and escaped this fate. Fortunately for him, everyone knew my father, so Dad visited the head of the army in Masindi at once and asked for my uncle's quick release.

Uncle Zulficar was not so lucky, he was murdered and left in his car with his head on the steering wheel near Fort Portal. The perpetrators tried to give the impression that he had committed suicide.

The cruelty intensified and it became impossible for Asians to remain in Uganda. Increasingly, people were forced to flee the country. My father and his brother, Uncle Hadi, decided that we, too, were left with no option but to leave. The army informed my father that they wished him to remain in the country and that they would provide protection for him.

CHAPTER 3

The Great Escape

Up until the "Asians out" declaration, my family had never travelled very far and had never felt any pressing need for a passport, which was already an essential document in the West. My father and mother were both born in Uganda, as were all their children. In Uganda, people did not have passports because they did not consider a need for one, and never envisioned circumstances in which they would require one. My mother did have one, but there was an issue, five of us children were on Mum's passport because we were under sixteen, but the eldest one, Shaida, who was over sixteen, did not have a passport.

There were long queues outside the British High Commission. With tensions growing daily, my family was particularly fearful for Shaida, as she was in a high-risk group susceptible to capture and rape by the soldiers. How could we get her out? We knew it would take days of queuing outside the passport office, and we did not want to take that chance. The streets were full of Amin's army, left to do whatever they wanted, so it became increasing difficult to survive from day to day. The army had also warned my father that if he were seen attempting to leave the country, they would shoot him. They needed him in Masindi for the shop, which provided them with luxury goods. Luckily, he was very good at keeping old documents, so he dug out my grandmother Jena's passport, which showed that she was born under British rule in India. This entitled my mother and her children to enter the UK.

The British were compassionate towards the young, and someone at the passport office suggested that for Shaida's safety, she should be dressed up, made to look 21, wear spectacles, and fly on the passport of my Aunt Begum, who had died in Mumbai. This would mean overriding the system. It was the only way to ensure Shaida's safety, even though we knew we would have to face consequences in the UK. What option were we left with?

It is well nigh impossible to describe the chaos that ensues when everyone wants to leave a country at once—or rather, is being forced out of it. There was simply no time to say farewell to friends and relatives. The streets were swarming with Amin's army. It was impossible for any Asian to wander around the streets without being stopped.

The first lot of Asians to leave Uganda were those who left for India; they drove to Kenya and then, via Mombasa, caught a ship to India. Very sadly, when visiting Goa many years later, I met an uncle, Navodia, who was amongst those first refugees. He was now paralysed. He told me that he had been working somewhere doing hard labour when something heavy had fallen on him and damaged his spine, from which he never recovered. His family had suffered severe poverty. This was just one of who knows how many sad and tragic outcomes following Amin's vile act. Years after the expulsion, Uncle Navodia passed away, followed by his wife, who passed away from an illness. Their daughter, Nargis, was the only survivor, and she recently died from an illness, too.

Despite the mounting fears and tensions in the wake of Amin's historic announcements, some people still went right to the wire in trying to guard their properties, but the army soon stripped them of any such rights. Amin even declared that anyone resisting the handing over of property should be shot. The army guarded seized properties, and it became obvious that these would eventually be given over to army officials.

In the meantime, people in the higher ranks in government were not happy with what was happening. They could see by then that Amin was not being fair to them. Colour became a big issue. One would be walking along a street when out of the blue, someone would say, "Wahindi (Asian), go back home." The whole atmosphere had changed. I should like to stress that there were many who remained opposed to Amin's rule and expulsion policy, but they were too frightened to speak out. These Ugandans did not want the Asians to suffer, and in some cases they were of great help by hiding some Asians amongst them. Ugandans on the whole are very gentle people, full of life and kindness. Others, though, were fed up with the idea of the Asians being such a big part of the economy—effectively controlling it—and every day newspapers would reproduce comments made by Amin, such as, "The Asians are milking the cow, but not feeding it." The Ugandans who read the newspapers learnt a lot more about the Asians and their alleged control of the economy.

However, this did not mean that the whole of the Asian race was covered in riches, or worked just for their own benefit. There were people like my father who truly believed in helping the whole of the human race, to improve their living standards, but as the saying goes, "The good goes with the bad, too". Idi Amin did not deal with this problem in a humane way because he was a mad and greedy man who not only wanted to throw the Asians out, but also wanted to destroy anyone who opposed him, at any cost. He did not have an economic strategy post the expulsion of the Asians.

Ahead of our own departure from the country, my father could not let anyone know that his family, and Uncle Hadi's family, were leaving the country, otherwise our lives would have been endangered. He pointedly took an evening walk around Masindi that particular evening, pretending for all to see that everything was completely normal. The plane tickets were purchased and held in advance by someone at the airport. My mother protested that she would not leave my father and uncle behind, but Dad succeeded in persuading her otherwise. Can you imagine how she must have felt? She was scared that something might happen to him and my uncles in our absence. But my father would not have it any other way. He had to come to the decision to get us to a safe haven.

Our last night at home in Masindi was very sad, my father told us that my mother, all my sisters, my brother, my aunt Farida and her daughter Shereena were leaving for England in just a few hours' time. Teresa and Raja, the two maids who had played a very big part in our upbringing, were hanging around to wave a final farewell to us. Teresa had been with us for many years and became a very big part of our family. She was a Munyoro, born and bred in Masindi, and she had a very motherly nature. Then there was Raja, who swapped around with Teresa's hours so that both could have time off. He was of the Nubian race, the same race as Idi Amin, but he totally opposed the Asian expulsion. These were two wonderful people who did not approve of Amin's reign and were very worried about what would happen to them when we left. All we heard from them was, "Please don't go, nothing will happen to you." That was fanciful thinking, of course.

We wondered what would happen to Dad and his brothers. How could we leave them behind? Would we ever see them again? These questions, and so many more, tormented us. What was happening to us was beyond belief. In a few hours, we would be leaving our home; but above all, we were going to be leaving my dad and his brothers. It felt like a bad dream. The cruel reality that we had been plunged into was horrendous.

At the crack of dawn, we woke up and saw a lorry arriving to pick us all up. I can still see the tears streaming from my mother's eyes—and from those of my father—as they said good-bye to each other. Dad stressed that if anything happened to him, Mum should look after the children, taking over the role of father, too, and carrying on with life to the best of her ability. She must not be defeated, he told her. My uncle Hadi was upset because he, too, was sending his family away with us—Aunt Farida and daughter, Shereena. Uncle Hadi had always faced tragedy in life; he had lost a son, Salim, who had died a few years back at a very young age. Uncle Sherali and Aunt Rashida were left behind, too, and we were terrified for them, they were practically newlyweds.

Clambering onto the lorry was like a scene out of a movie. Raja gave my father a helping hand in transferring us into the back of the vehicle. Being able to hear gunfire in the near distance did not help our nerves. As the lorry drove off, I remember us all waving to my father and uncles, with their images becoming ever smaller as the distance between us increased. Eventually, all we could see as we looked back was the Kigulia hill that embraced my home.

The whole experience was incredibly emotional. We had left without any possessions, except the clothes we were wearing, but that was not a concern at that moment. We were stopped at many points by the army; there were barriers everywhere. We were hiding in the back of the vehicle, frozen with fear and warned to be totally silent. The driver, who had known my father for a long time, was very loyal and very cool—and he needed to be. He would draw to a halt and act normally when questioned, giving no cause for suspicion, and so we were let through every barrier. Each time a barricade was cleared, we would breathe a great sigh of relief until the next one. At each barrier, the soldiers would ask our driver where he was heading while pointing a gun at him, and he would reply, "Going to Kampala to purchase some goods." They always let him pass through. Any other outcome—with soldiers deciding to search the vehicle—simply didn't bear contemplating, and even now it sends a shiver down my spine whenever I think about it. We were so frightened and panic stricken. If any of my brother or sisters had to cough, my mother would cover their mouths with her hand—otherwise the consequences would have been lethal.

As we drove through the Ugandan countryside, the sun was rising and full daylight was emerging. At one point, as we passed a barrier, we saw several dead bodies in the distance. We heard from the driver that the driver of the vehicle ahead of us had got into an argument with the soldiers at the barrier, and they had shot him, and his passengers, dead. There was absolutely no law and order, and the soldiers were behaving in whatever manner pleased them.

Chapter 4

A New Country, and the Start of Our New Lives

Our arrival at Entebbe Airport was another weird experience. Although we had been born and brought up in Uganda, until now we didn't even have a clue where Entebbe was. We emerged from the lorry very tired after a six-hour journey, and we headed towards the airport terminal, where we were treated like criminals. Our bodies and clothing were checked to see if we were hiding any money. We were manhandled extremely roughly—for some reason, they even found cause to scratch their fingers through our hair, presumably to make sure that we had not hidden anything there!

We were put in queues holding our passports. The immigration officers were not exactly polite; all they wanted was to see the back of us.

There was a massive queue for emigration, and once that process had been concluded, we were herded into another queue for vaccinations. Anyone travelling to the UK had to have this immunisation. In those days, they did not use a new needle for each individual, and you could actually see that the needle was blunt by the time it got to the tenth person. As permanent testimony to this, I have a mark on my right arm that is shaped like a five-pence coin. I have not had it removed because it constantly reminds me of who I am and what I overcame.

There were all sorts of checks prior to our flight out from Entebbe. I saw a lady whose hair was pulled apart because she had tied it up in a French bun. In the far distance, I saw an officer pulling off a bracelet from a passenger, but no one could do anything except keep quiet, get onto the plane safely and count one's blessings. I remember thinking to myself, "This much punishment, just for being Asian?"

We were marched to the plane under police escort. As we got on, none of us even knew what a plane would look like inside. My little brother Ferride was excited because my father had bought him toy planes on his birthdays, and he was very fond of them. Now he was about to witness the real thing! He was too young to understand what was actually happening. We took our seats and were asked to fasten our seat belts. Again, this was all new territory for us. Who amongst us would have known how to fasten these things? It was kind of funny, upon reflection, because in the West a child of three would know how to fasten a seat belt. An air stewardess showed us all how to do it.

By the time we had boarded, it was evening. It had been such a long day, first with the long journey and then with all the hassle at the airport. Everyone was very quiet and found it hard to come to terms with the whole experience.

And so, some nine hours later, my new life began with the airplane touching down at Stansted Airport in England, to the northeast of London. This was the UK's third largest airport, after Heathrow and Gatwick, and its terminal building was just three years old when we arrived there. One could imagine what a contrast that was compared with the facilities we had left behind. The airport buildings were truly glittering affairs compared with Entebbe.

For all its newness, it was a very scary time for me as a young child, arriving in what for me was a whole new world, having been uprooted in truly terrifying manner from everything that was familiar to me. Not that I knew it at the time—and not that it would have been any comfort—but we were helping make a little bit of history here for the second time in a quarter of a century. In the late 1940s, after the Second World War, Stansted was used for housing German prisoners of war. Now here we were, thousands in all, flying in from our beloved Uganda.

It was an early morning arrival in the month of October, and so the immediately noticeable difference for us was that it was cold and very misty. Like so much else that was happening to us then, this was an entirely new experience to us; we had never known cold winters. We disembarked and were guided to the immigration office, where we had to queue up in the Commonwealth section. We were asked for our vaccination documents, and there were volunteers who helped us with the English language. Most of us could speak some English, albeit not with a very British accent, but we could come across reasonably well except for the elderly, who could only speak a few words such as "please" and "thank you". We were then all X-rayed, one by one, to make sure that we were well and not bringing in any diseases.

As we were queuing, I remember people in the other queues staring at us. I assumed that by now the whole world had heard of the Ugandan Asian expulsion, and here they were in the presence of some of us—the people of the moment, in current affairs terms. Consider the sight we presented. There we were, early in the morning on a day in the middle of October, dressed just in our summer clothes and shoes with no jackets.

There were some Indian volunteers who were trained to help the aged with their language problems. These volunteers then guided us to the buses that were going to take us to our camp. At this point, for the first time in my life, I heard the word "refugee". Until then none of us had known the meaning of the word; as time went on, we were left in no doubt as to what it actually meant.

After a four-hour drive we arrived at the camps at Gaydon, near Leamimgton Spa in Warwickshire. By this time it was night, and we were handed over to more volunteers. The buildings looked big and strange; I would liken them to a block of warehouses, grey with big windows. We were then marched to a Red Cross building where we were asked to queue. Ahead of our arrival, the public had been asked to donate coats and other warm clothing that was no longer of any use to them but which could be vital to us. We were asked to select winter coats and jumpers. There was no system of measurement. We just tried a coat on, and if it fitted, then fine, and if it did not then, we would try on more until we got the nearest fit. We were so cold that nothing else mattered; even if we had been given a sack to wear, we would have accepted it with gratitude in order to be able to protect ourselves from the cold. I remember clearly my poor mother struggling with my younger brother and sisters in the queue. My aunt was hanging onto her daughter.

Insofar as I can remember it, we all looked lost, depressed, and hurt. We were given numbers to our dormitories; ours was number eleven. These dormitories looked like hospital wards, with many beds on either side. At the end of the dormitory was a toilet to be shared by everyone.

By everyone—there were around eight toilets and bathrooms in the camp—to be shared by some five hundred people. Not surprisingly, the toilets were filthy.

Here we joined many other families from Uganda. It became a sort of a village for many weeks. My mother and aunt were very tearful, not just because of the traumatic experience but because they were worried for my father and uncles' wellbeing. We were going through a truly horrible upheaval—it was something one just couldn't imagine unless one had actually been through it.

As well as the bigger picture, there were the little things, such as being given corn flakes to eat for breakfast. None of us knew what these crisp, flaky things were or how we were supposed to eat them. The staff, demonstrating with their spoons and jugs of milk, had to explain it to us! We were also offered fresh bread rolls and eggs, of which we became very fond. But it was all so very different from what we were used to. It didn't take us long to learn about the English diet. The one thing that we could not get over was the fact that we had been separated from my father, uncles, and aunt. I observed my mum many times, and she was miles away in thought and sometimes very tearful. She was obviously missing my dad and confronting her own thoughts of whether she would ever see him again, what life would be like without him, and where she would be heading next?

We found life very difficult at the army camp. The staff, I am sure, did an excellent job and could not have been more helpful, but it was all such a huge change in our lives. For one thing, it felt so cold in the English autumn, and I had never worn a coat before; it felt so heavy and uncomfortable. One minute we had been living in a private house in our native land, and the next we were in a dormitory, sharing with other families and living in a very strange, new land. And to see my mother suffering so much, without my father and with so many children to take care of, most of them younger than me—it was a truly painful experience.

In our dormitory, everyone had to wake up at the same time, around seven o'clock, in order to queue for breakfast. The queues were long—especially outside the bathrooms and toilets. For all that, we were all very self-disciplined; no one tried to jump those queues. Everyone was still in a state of shock at what had happened to him or her. If anything, this shock only served to bring us all closer together. After breakfast, we could go to some offices that had been converted into schools to help us learn English. There were all sorts of groups, from beginners to those who were pretty fluent. These English lessons would be followed by lunch, when occasionally the staff would be kind enough to cook the sort of curries to which we were accustomed. They weren't entirely like the real thing back home, but we certainly appreciated their efforts. Indeed, the volunteers were very kind to us; they would constantly ask if we were okay, or if we needed extra blankets. Every family was given £2.10 per week for personal use. I remember a Mr Patel, across from us in the dormitory, who was overjoyed because he was a smoker and now he could buy cigarettes for himself. He was there with his wife and his two daughters.

Some days there would be minibuses laid on in the afternoons to take us to Leamington Spa, for us to look at the shops. I remember telling one of the staff who had accompanied us that I was really craving some chocolate. When I boarded the minibus again for the return journey, I discovered that she had gone and bought a couple of big bars of Cadbury's, which she shared with us. It was delicious, and it was so kind of her. I could not praise the staff too highly.

I have been back to Leamington Spa in the last couple of years, and it still has a sense of belonging. It has expanded a great deal since my first visits to it, but the streets felt the same—especially the high street, where I could picture my mother crossing the road whilst ensuring that all six of us joined her in total safety. I remember my brother Ferride, who was a typical boy, running across the road without looking—resulting in my poor mother having to shout at him for fear that he would one day be run over.

My mother missed my father so much, as we all did. She was very good at knitting, so she was provided with wool and spent a lot of time making hats and gloves for us, and, it seemed, everyone else, too. She was very strong mentally. On many occasions, we would ask her about Dad. Although she could not be sure of the outcome, she would convince us that he would be well and that we would be reunited with him soon. She never gave up—she was strong, just like her own mother.

Chapter 5

England

We gradually got used to our new way of life, until one day my uncle Hassan came to fetch us. He had been in England a bit longer than we had. We learned of my twin uncles' time in England before we arrived. Their strength and hard work was a true sign of their love for us, but how could that not be, because they had Grandad's and Grandma's blood running through their veins. When they arrived in the UK, they were sent to a camp at Honiton, Devon. They had been there for three weeks when my uncle Valimohammad and his son, Alinaki, took them to Neasden, North London. Alinaki was one of the pioneers who introduced cassava to the UK market. Cassava is a vegetable grown underground like potatoes, and it is a very special diet for Africans, Asians also having acquired a taste for it.

Valimohammad Mama; his wife, Laila Mami, and their lovely family Alinaki, Mohsin, Nazma, Modisa, Fatma, Ali Raza and Rozy were very close to us. Mama was a very kind and gentle soul, a very good humanitarian who always gave to charity in whatever way he could.

My uncle Hassan was only 19 years old, which was an incredibly young age to be harbouring such responsibility for us all. I must admit, as we left the camp to travel to London by British Rail, accompanied by uncle Hassan, and said good-bye to all the volunteers; we looked thoughtfully at those who were left behind. Only God knew how long they would remain there. We had been living with these people for a while and had become very close to them, like one large family. I remember a very elderly gentleman who had lost his wife and was in the camp with his only son. As we were leaving, he asked us to take both him and his son with us. It was a sad sight because we had to leave him behind—we weren't sure of our own destiny, so how could we possibly help anyone else?

We arrived in Balham, South London, where uncle Hassan had rented a three-storey, seven-bedroom room house for forty pounds a week. We were very excited to be reunited with our grandmother and Aunt Laila. The number of occupants increased to fifteen. It was also a very cold house with high ceilings and a fireplace in the front room, but I'm sure our strength of family unit added a warmth of its own. Outside, there was a little garden with washing lines.

On that train journey from the camp to London, we were unfortunate enough to suffer our first experience of racism. A young, and well-dressed, man started to shout, "Go back to your own country." We didn't understand what he meant, but a lady sitting next to my mum started to defend us and told him off. I remember her face; she was a beautiful, young English woman. She had a right go at him, saying, "Don't you think these people have been through enough in life? Look at these poor children." She shut him up, thank God, and we realised then that there are good and bad people in every race. We were able to ignore this incident.

We were, and still are, a very close family then. The twin uncles and my aunt worked and brought in the money while Mum, Grandmother and the other aunt took care of the household chores. We had one small black-and-white television set, and we would all happily sit around it every evening and pray together. Materialistic things did not matter, so long as we had food on the table. We enjoyed a very special bond with my grandmother. She loved us so much that we felt certain that she would even sacrifice her own life for us if ever she had to. Ferride, my brother, was the only boy, so Grandma understandably spoilt him. My mother also loved him deeply. We never resented this, because all his sisters adored him, too—a very gentle soul.

Following our move to Balham, a Mr Jones from the local Department of Social Security office visited us every week to review our welfare. He arranged for the education authority to get in touch with us so that we could be put in local schools. Shaida, my eldest sister, was lucky because she got into a Clapham grammar school, and I went to Garratt Green Secondary School, all the others went to Graveny, South London.

We very gratefully received a UK government grant for school uniforms and shoes. I remember Mr Jones as a very nice, extremely helpful man who was very kind at heart and had such a gentle soul. It was so apparent that he wanted to help us. In fact, my father stayed in touch with him down the years, and we always received a Christmas card from him, even when he had retired. I hated Garratt Green at first, it was huge school and some of the girls were very unkind. Children can be so cruel to each other, and these girls would laugh at the poor quality of our shoes, because we could not afford decent ones. We would also have our English accent mocked because it still had a foreign touch about it. There was no denying that these were very difficult days. If we had holes in our shoes, we would not tell our mother because we knew she would feel bad and would want to buy a new pair—but there just wasn't enough money and it would have been unfair to ask.

Although there were already fifteen of us in that house, it would become even more crowded with occasional guests. My grandmother was always very generous and would never turn a fly away, so any relative who was stranded over here from Uganda would come and stay with us for long periods. We would just put mattresses on the floor and make do as best we could. My mother and grandmother would cook, clean, wash, iron, and generally look after the household. There was not enough money for adequate heating, so we would turn on the heaters for a little while and then Mum and Grandma would make hot water bottles for everyone. There were six of us in Mum's bedroom, with one double bed and the rest of us sleeping on mattresses on the ground. Our visitors included my lovely Aunt Nabat; her husband, Amir bhai; her daughter, Femida, and her son, Alikhan. She was my dad's first cousin and was a very gentle soul who helped a lot around the house with the chores. They eventually decided to settle in Canada.

Bahdur Bhai Gillani was a very gentle soul, his wife Gulshan Bhai and their daughter Lailla visited often, they were like a family who helped us a lot too.

My poor twin uncles, Hassan and Hussein, deferred their studies by one year and worked for K Shoe shops (now part of Clarks) and my Aunt Laila worked for Barclays Bank. We knew that as long as there was a big family bond, which there was, we could fight anything.

As an amusing aside, my uncle Hassan was in a desperate need of a job, so someone he met told him that there were posters on Oxford Street advertising modelling opportunities. Well, he didn't have a clue about modelling and what it entailed, but off he went. He was asked to strip in order to show off his biceps. He obviously needed a fit body and lots of working out if he was going to become a successful model. The poor fellow was mightily embarrassed and took off quickly.

We had one big shopping trip every week—strictly no luxuries, just the bare necessities. Conventional heating bills were out of the question; there was only just enough money to buy the food to keep us alive. As well as feeding and heating us, Mum and Grandma would wash all our clothes. They did this in cold water—firstly, because there was no washing machine, and secondly because to heat the water was just too expensive. Their hands would be frozen by the time they finished washing all the clothes. I remember feeling their hands once, and finding them rough and tired. However, even with their rough hands, when they embraced me I felt like I was in heaven and the worries of the world went away.

Chapter 6

Agreement

Meanwhile, we were still in the midst of trying to locate the whereabouts of my missing father and uncles, and after another few months we were finally reunited with them. It began when we heard on the radio that those Asians who had been left stateless in Uganda had been airlifted out of the country by the United Nations, and taken to countries such as Italy, Austria, and Switzerland.

My father obviously knew that we were somewhere in Britain, so he sent a letter through someone who was with him at his base in Austria, who also had family in the UK. One day there was a knock on our door and a gentleman by the name of Alizaman handed over this letter from my father. One could not imagine the joy on our faces, especially Mum, Baa, and Aunt Farida. Until then we hadn't even known if Dad was still alive, let alone where he was. Now we had confirmation that he was alive.

The negotiations began. My father and his brothers, we learnt, were living in Austria, in a beautiful little town called Wallsee, surrounded by mountains. The letter was a huge morale booster with the confirmation that Dad was in good health and being treated well. He subsequently told us that the people there were wonderful and he had made great friends. The Austrian Government had put them up in hotels and gave them money. There was a shop near where Dad was staying where he regularly purchased daily newspapers to keep in touch with world events.

It was through negotiations of Prince Sadruddin Aga Khan that the last remaining refugees were airlifted to Austria and other European countries. Prince Sadruddin Aga Khan had became a special envoy to the United Nations High Commissioner for Refugees (UNHCR) in 1959. Seven years later, in 1966, he became the High Commissioner—becoming the youngest person (at the age of just 33) to be appointed.

I simply cannot express too strongly my gratitude to him for his role in helping my father. Without his help, my father and Uncle Hadi Kaka would not have made it to the UK.

At the same time, there were debates going on in the UK Parliament over whether the men stranded in Austria and elsewhere, without their families, should be accepted by Britain or be resettled elsewhere in the world. Edward Heath (later Sir Edward) was Prime Minister, and Robert Carr (later Lord Carr) was Home Secretary.

In Austria, Prince Sadruddin visited the refugees in Wallsee where, with the Prince's kind permission, my father made a speech. He stood up and addressed a good three hundred people. He said that people with families living elsewhere in the world would be indescribably grateful if arrangements could be made for them to be reunited. On behalf of himself and all the other refugees in Austria, Dad also expressed his immense gratitude to the Austrian Government for their kindness in allowing them into that country and looking after them so well. He had special thanks for the Prince for making time—so much appreciated considering his busy schedule—to visit all refugees and address their problems.

Back in the UK, after seemingly endless negotiations, we were watching the BBC news one evening when we heard that the British parliament had agreed to accept those refugees who had families already in the UK. We were overjoyed for my father and Uncle Hadi—although this was tempered by great sadness and concern for Uncle Sherali and Aunty Rashida. They were stranded in Austria, without any family, and we did not know what would happen to them.

Aunty Rashida's brother, Shiraz, was already in Canada, and sponsored Uncle Sherali and Aunty Rashida for emigration to Canada. In the meantime, Dad and Uncle Hadi were reunited with us in the UK, and so we were able to resume life as a complete family unit. This was around June of 1973. There is only one word to describe that experience and all the emotions we felt at that moment, as Dad and Hadi rejoined us in our house:—amazing. Tears of joy streamed down all our faces. Even my little brother ran to Dad and grabbed him, clutching him with all the strength at his disposal. The joy was expressed not least by Baa. She had left her three sons in Uganda, not knowing if she would ever see them again in this life and no doubt fearing the worst. What an amazing ending to that chapter in our lives; it was truly mind-blowing and with Gods grace.

CHAPTER 7

New Foundations, More Moves

Soon it was time for Dad and Uncle Hadi to move on, even when the two of them had lost motivation and were beginning to drown in sadness of what had happened. We were going to school every day and my aunt and uncles were already in work. We could not live in rented council accommodation forever—we had to start looking ahead. For starters, we recognised and accepted that going back to Uganda would not be possible, that it was very much a closed chapter.

Uncle Hadi and his family moved to Rawtenstall, Lancashire. Uncle Hadi found himself a job there, working as a postman and he was able to support himself and his family. One of Dad's sisters, Roshan, and her husband, Fidai, along with their three children, Hanif, Shams, and Rahim, had been located in Lancashire after expulsion from Uganda. They were taken to another camp in the north and then advised to settle there by the Settlement Board.

Dad was trying very hard to find a business within his means. By the grace of God, he found a little late night, seven-day-week grocery shop that was for sale in Balham—near the tube and railway stations—which was run by our landlord, Mansur Charania. Over many weeks, he observed the shop and concluded that it needed two people to run it. He got in touch with Uncle Hadi and asked him if he would like to come and join him in what would be a new family business. Dad explained that it would only work if there were no wage costs, because the takings weren't enough to pay staff wages—but it needed another family member to help with the hours and the workload. Dad succeeded in persuading Uncle Hadi to give up his job and bring his family back to Balham. The shop was on Chestnut Grove, opposite a school were my brother Ferride and younger sisters Sahera, Shamira and Naffilla attended. There was a flat above the shop that we all moved to, but that was not big enough, and so we rented the flat next door. Dad, my uncle and our families remained in the flat above the shop, but Baa, the twin uncles and Aunty Laila moved to the flat next door.

We did not renew the house tenancy agreement because my twin uncles had gone back to studying and we could not afford the expensive accommodation anymore, costing £40 a week. I was not at all happy about our move into these flat over the shop—in fact, I hated it! Our flat was so small and the fact that it was just across the road from the railway station meant that we could hear the trains as early as five o'clock in the morning, which meant a premature end to a nice night's sleep. At least the house we had rented had a garden; this flat had none and was so crowded.

Everyone worked extremely hard. My grandmother would help in the shop every afternoon, standing beside Dad and Uncle Hadi at the counter. This was designed to take account of children from the school across the road who tried their hand at shoplifting. Grandma had a very sharp eye for such activity. My mother and aunt would look after the children and my mum would cook for everyone.

My father made sure that we all watched the 9.00 p.m. news on the BBC; this was compulsory for all of us. At the time, I thought my father was being unreasonably strict, but as I grew up I came to realise just how important it was to know what was going on around us and in the world. This awareness was a very important part of education.

My dad and Uncle Hadi would work seven days a week, from 7.00 a.m. to 8.00 p.m. They would only take off one Sunday every fortnight. We used to stick cinema advertisement posters in the shop window, and in return we would have two free Bollywood film tickets. We would all take turns in going. That was such fun, looking forward to a film. One's turn would only come every eight weeks. That's a stark comparison between life then and now. Today I could see a film at the cinema every day if I wanted to, but after a long day's work, I much prefer to sit in front of the TV, in the comfort of my own home. The income from the shop was not good at the beginning, at least not in terms of how much was required to support so many people. It was asking a great deal of this one little shop to provide the money to feed so many mouths.

Hassan and Hussein had to stop working at this point and return to education; they had always wanted to become accountants. Aunt Laila, who had been a teacher at the sought after Gayaza High School in Kampala, got a job in a bank. Dad would go to the cash and carry twice a week to buy the goods for the shop, and Hadi Kaka would look after the shop. It was such hard work. I used to feel so sorry when I saw Dad huffing and puffing after a heavy day at the cash and carry and my uncle would be exhausted after unloading all the goods.

Hassan and Hussein went to Brighton to study and they also found life very difficult. They were staying in a single rented room. The landlords, Mr & Mrs Lawson, occasionally allowed them to watch Top of the Pops in the living room. With money so scarce, they had to make do with severely limited food options. Sometimes, if they ran out of money altogether, they would just make do with butter and a loaf of bread between the pair of them. They were aware that the whole family was struggling financially, and so it was only later that we learnt just how difficult these times had been for them—despite their own predicament, they had gone out of their way to avoid putting extra pressure on us. They knew that on completion of their education, which was the most important thing for them at the time, they would be able to earn a lot more and help the family.

I continued my education at Garrat Green, but I also became a bit of a naughty young lady! In those days, catalogues would come through the door much more so than they do now, and I would use them to order clothes. I thought I would be able to pay for them from the little bit of pocket money I received from my parents. When it became apparent that I could not meet these payments, my parents would receive court summons, and they would get angry with me. This happened twice, and Dad paid the fines in court. After the second time, he came home and made a point of showing me his pair of shoes. He stared at me, looking really upset, and turned his shoes upside down in front of me. In clear view was a great big hole in one of them. That was a measure of the family's financial situation, he explained. He was just about making ends meet, he added, and if only I would stop buying things through a catalogue, our affairs might improve. I felt so upset and angry with myself. There was my father, who denied himself something pretty much essential in order to save money for the benefit of his family, and there I was buying things I didn't need. I promised myself from that day onwards that I would prove to my parents that I would be a good child, like their other children. I got myself a Saturday job in the perfume department at Harrods in Kensington, and I used my own money to buy whatever I wanted. My eldest sister, Shaida, had been doing a Saturday job since the age of fifteen, working for British Home Stores in Tooting Broadway, and it seemed only fair that I should do the same.

We also had a bigger TV set now that operated using a coin slot, which required regular feeding for continuous viewing. If there was no change left, and we were in the middle of watching a programme, then that was it—we lost that programme and would all disperse quietly to our rooms. Our Balham shop's takings increased after a few months, and things generally got better. Around the 1980, my dad was able to buy a house on Pretoria Road, Streatham. This was a very comfortable, three-bedroom, terraced house. We received lots of visitors here. We would all have breakfast together when Dad had his Sunday off. I spent some very happy teenage years there. I shared a downstairs bedroom with Sahera and Shamira.

Dad and his brothers diversified into the property market and prospered through hard work. My mother worked at the Gloucester Road Hotel as an assistant in the housekeeping department. She would leave home early and return before we got back from school. Our food would be ready and waiting for us, as would our school uniforms for the next morning. Although life was improving materially, it was still not easy. Down the road in Streatham, the community had hired a hall for prayer, and we attended almost every day. Religion always offered comfort, and it was good to spend time out reassuring ourselves of the ultimate; it kind of brought us back to the ground, for want of a better expression. Here we made lots of friends and helped each other in whatever way possible. We had a sense of belonging to this community—something we had been very used to back in Uganda. The belief in God was embedded into us from childhood, and this is what pulled us through bad times.

Chapter 8

Family Moves

Shaida finished her basic education and went on to study for the Institute of Accounting Staff qualification, eventually clinching a job at the Gloucester Road Hotel, where Mum worked. Shaida was a good girl and would offer her wages to Mum and Dad to help them out, but they refused to take them and encouraged her to save money.

When she was about twenty and studying at Waltham Forest College she met a very handsome young man called Nizam. He was studying to be a motor mechanic. Shaida was very friendly with Nizam's sister, Shenaz, who we got very close to as a family due to her splendid nature. Nizam's parents, my Aunty Sakar and Uncle Fateh, were incredible people. Shaida started to date Nizam, but in those days things were slightly different. When Nizam took her out, he would be dating not only her, but also the whole clan. The couple would also be accompanied by all my other sisters and brother. As well as the inconvenience, this would also work out costly for him, the poor guy. He would take her out to the cinema with the whole clan and end up paying for popcorn and ice cream during the interval. He was very generous and never complained.

Nizam proposed to Shaida within five months of meeting her, and they were married ten months later in a nice, small wedding above the Satander Bank in Balham. In those days the weddings were not as expensive as what they are today. After many years of hard work, they ended up buying a garage business in Balham. Shaida worked with

Nizam for a number of years and educated their two children. Their children, Nabilla and Imran, are very close to us, and we have shared a lot of good and bad times with them.

When Nabilla, who we called Nabs, was born, she was the first grandchild for my parents and we were so overjoyed. She brought so much joy and a new beginning to our lives. We would all buy her toys and frocks. Today Nabs is married to a lovely German chap, Jan, and works for Boris Johnson, the Lord Mayor of London. Nabs has just given birth to her second child Raiyan Benjamin and also has a two-year-old daughter, Hanna Sophia—a very cute little girl whom we rally around. Imran, my nephew who was the second born, is a dentist based in Bristol and is married to Kristina, a Bristolian who is also a dentist. They have a new arrival Luca, a lovely little boy.

Nizam played a very fatherly role to us siblings. Because he saw us all growing up through hardships and pressures and we grew up with him, he became a very big part of our lives. Shenaz and I became the best of friends and I missed her very much when she got married to Amir and moved to America. She now lives in Atlanta with Amir and their son, Noorez. Nizam has another sister, Shairoz, who lives with her family in Edmonton. He has extended family in London too, his wadima, cousin Mohammad, Malek, and their family, with whom I have always had a great bond and shared special occasions.

Dad continued with the shop in Balham, and with his brothers eventually bought another shop across the road in 1978. This was a fruit shop with a flat above. Uncle Akbar, who had just qualified as a land surveyor at Nairobi University, moved to London and got married to Naseem. He helped with the shop for a little while and was then advised by his brothers to move to Canada, which was more beneficial for his career. He moved to Edmonton and settled there.

Things improved financially and as time went on all the brothers invested in more properties. By the 1980s market values were soaring. We all continued with our studies. I took my A-levels and then had a gap year. My brother Ferride went to Brighton to study pharmacy. He worked extremely hard, and when I look back today, my heart fills with sadness because he was the only boy and always had to prove himself to the others. Sahera, Shamira, and Naffilla were all still at school. They were so content and never asked for more, like the teenagers of today. They wore whatever Mum bought them and were very happy souls. I sometimes look back at life and wish I could go back in time, so I could protect them even more than I did. I remember their little faces reflect how my sisters and brother missed my father when we were in the camp. All of them would toss and turn during the night, missing Dad and not knowing what was happening to them. Now we just live with precious memories of him since we lost him through cancer. Dad will always remain embedded in our hearts.

One can imagine what Ferride must have gone through, being the only brother amongst five sisters. He was always a very gentle soul and he never had his own way. My grandmother and my parents cherished him, although they never spoilt him, but he was the apple of my grandmother's eye. You could see a twinkle in her eye when she looked at him. He loved her dearly. Ferride would visit us every weekend after going away to Brighton. We always teased him about girls because he was always putting his head down and working hard. However, he shocked us one day! He asked my mum to organise a party for his fellow students at our house in Streatham, and he invited a number of guests for New Year's celebrations—including a young lady with whom he was friendly. The next day he asked Mum and Dad what we had thought of this young lady, Parminer Kaur (Pam). Clearly, Mum and Dad had gathered by now why he was so keen to know. In no time at all, we heard that he wanted to marry her. However, there were complications. My brother was Muslim and Pam was a devout Sikh.

Things have changed a lot since then and some things that were unacceptable 30 years ago are no longer so. My father was always very open-minded and accepted anyone with open arms. Ferride and Pam eloped and faced a lot of issues that took a long time to sort out. They lived with my parents for a while and gave them a lovely grandson, a very dear nephew of mine, Waseem. We were so overjoyed, he brought so much excitement to our lives, especially my dad's. Dad would look at him and call him Dr Waseem Karsan—he wanted a couple of his grandchildren to become doctors and help save lives. As I write this today, Waseem is a newly qualified, Prague educated medical doctor fulfilling my father's dream. Twenty members of the family shared a great few days in Prague attending Waseem's graduation. We missed Dad, but I am sure he was there in spirit with us.

Ferride and Pam then had two more lovely daughters—Yasmin, who is a pharmacist, and Shabnam, who is studying to be one. Then they had another boy, Salman, who is a fine young man but is very much the baby of the family. After Waseem's birth, Ferride's family moved to Rochester, Kent, where he has his own businesses. With the grace of God, they settled very well in that county. They each run their own pharmacies. My brother was recently nominated as one of the best businessmen in Rochester by locals; citing his kindness towards his customers and going the extra mile to help humanity.

After my father's death in 2006, this brother and my sister-in-law have played a major part in looking after the family. Ferride has very much become a father figure and is even beginning to look like my dad. My father loved Pam like his own daughter and she has always done her best for the family. There was an incident when Pam had a very difficult delivery giving birth to my youngest nephew, Salman. My father and mother rushed off to the hospital, and Pam told us that she could hear my father telling the doctors that if he could give up his life for her to be saved, he would. She always tells us that she saw him as a caring father who would do anything for his children and grandchildren.

Pam has just lost her dear mother too, a gentle soul leaving behind a devoted family and her soul mate, Pam's father.

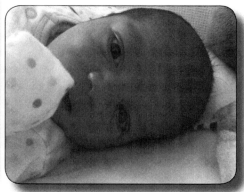

Miss Hana Sophia Stelter and Master Raiyan Benjamin Stelter
half-German, half-Indian.

Master Luca Nasser
half-English, half-Indian.

Zahra, Yasmin, Roshan [grandma] Farzana, Shabnam.

Dr. Waseem Karsan, Salman Karsan, Karim Nanji.

CHAPTER 9

My Year in India

My parents were actually not happy for me to go to India because they wanted me to continue with my education, but somehow I was able to persuade them. I really wanted to travel to the East and learn a lot about my ancestors. My sister, Sahera, and my cousin, Shams, accompanied me. It was the first time I had been abroad since I left Uganda. We landed in Mumbai, a beautiful Maharastrian vibrant city full of hustle and bustle, where the shops are open all hours. I had watched a lot of Bollywood films, but I had given no thought to what I was going to see when we landed there.

My aunt Shirin lived in Andheri, which was not a long way from the Chhatrapati Shivaji International Airport in Santa Cruz, but the journey was a real eye-opener. The rows of corrugated iron sheet houses were so different from the concrete blocks of England; it brought back the memories of when I lived in Masindi Port. The taxi driver dropped us outside my aunt's house and our holiday began. At first the country's poverty really got to us. The only poverty that we had previously experienced was when we were children in Uganda. In a way it was good that we should have this fresh exposure, because it reminded us once more that there were millions of people around the world who knew nothing other than the pain of hunger—yet they could smile and be happy. We had taken lots of pens and pencils and some other stationery and toys to hand out to children who on receiving the goods were overjoyed.

Aunt Shirin's husband, Masa, was working at that time for Film Laya Studios. We were teenagers and were crazy about meeting Bollywood stars. We stayed with them for a week, and Masa took us to watch loads of studio film shootings.

At the same time, our dear Uncle Valimohammad Mama and Laila Mami were visiting India and staying at the Seagreen Hotel in Mumbai, which is at Nariman Point. They had gone to Mumbai for the wedding of their son Aliraza (one of my favourite uncles). We spent a lovely week with them.

Before we took off to Gujarat, where my grandparents originated from, we had some important matters to attend to in Mumbai. We had to visit my aunt Begum's grave, she had a hole in hear heart and had passed at the young age of 23 during heart surgery. She was born in Uganda and was an avid student; she did however have to struggle with lots of absence due to her condition. She was in desperate need of an operation and was admitted many times to Mulago hospital in Kampala, one of the foremost medical institutions in Uganda, However, she was not able to get the surgery she needed, as it was very specialised at that time. The family could not afford to pay for specialist care. After many years had passed the family managed to save up enough money for surgical intervention at Mumbai hospital, one of the few in the world offering such surgery at that time.

My aunt Choti kindly offered to share her one room in Hassanabagh, Mazagaon, in Mumbai, with my dad and aunt, there was very limited space in this one room, as it was already housing Choti's family, so my dad had to sleep on a bench outside aunt Choti who was incredible humanitarian. Before aunt Begum was admitted to the hospital, she asked Dad to take her shopping so she could buy gifts for everyone back home in Uganda. She wanted very much to take them back and bestow them upon the family once she had recovered from her operation, however this was not meant to be. She was in high spirits upon admission to the hospital and was given a very good chance, as much as 90 percent.

The operation lasted for 18 hours and throughout Dad never left the observation room at the theatre. The operation went quite smoothly and she was moved into a recovery room, she opened her eyes and told my dad that she felt ok, and told him to return home to freshen up, he could always return in the evening, which he did. On his way he stopped to buy her some flowers and chocolates overzealously happy to see her in good health, but as he approached the recovery room back at the hospital there was lots of activity in and out of the room, when he tried to enter, but hospital staff stopped him. A few minutes later, a doctor came from the recovery room and told my dad that she had suffered a massive heart attack, which she had not survived. My dad was completely grief stricken and heartbroken with the loss of his sister, he was alone.

Aunt Choti went to great lengths to help him arrange the funeral and auntie Begum was laid to rest in Mumbai. On the flight home, my father did not speak, stuck in a cold numbness at the loss of his sister. My grandparents were also emotionally devastated at the loss, and just two years later my grandfather, who had suffered greatly in silence, also passed away. My grandmother mentioned Aunt Begum every single day until she herself passed away it was a tragic scar on my family's history that has never healed. After putting all my own affairs in order, I left Mumbai and the sorrow I had endured to visit other parts of India, starting off with my grandfather's village.

First we visited his village, Sanosra, which still had all of three houses. Charming old gentlemen of around 90, called Bhura Bhai, came out to greet us when he saw our car. We tried to explain who we were, and once we named my grandfather, this kind man became so excited, explaining that he knew my grandfather when he was 16. He asked me how my grandfather was, and it was my sad duty to tell him that he was no longer alive. Bhura Bhai said my grandfather had promised him that he would return to India to visit this village, but he never did. My grandfather had left the village to go to Uganda with his brothers Abji and Shivji. Tears rolled down his face as he told me that my grandfather was one of the finest men that he had ever known, and that he was present at his wedding.

Masi, the wife of Bhura Bhai, also came out, and she laid out the bed that was outside the house. It had no mattress but she put a red piece of velvet material on it for us to sit down on. I tried to stop her by sitting on the floor, but she refused and insisted that we all sit on the bed. She made Indian tea, which tasted amazing and was made with alichi and cardamoms and served in little vessels of clay. Bhura Bhai took us around the farm where he grew mustard seeds and corn. This was what my grandfather and his brothers used to do while they were in India—they were farmers. I walked for miles around the farm, the greenery and the fresh air. Above all the hospitality made me feel like I never wanted to leave.

When the time came to say farewell, Bhura Bhai and his wife gave me a red handkerchief and some money for us to share. At first I refused to take the money, but this clearly offended them and so I accepted it with great pride. The handkerchief is still with me today, and to say I treasure it is an understatement.

The welcome I had received from this couple was incredible. It felt as if they were a part of my family and that I had enjoyed a bond with them for a whole lifetime. Unfortunately, I received a letter from his wife a few years ago informing me that Bhura Bhai was no longer with us. I was very saddened by this news because it meant that I had lost not only a dear friend but also a link with someone who had grown up with my grandfather.

After Sanosra, my journey took us to my grandmother's village, Sindavadar, in Gujarat. This was a very picturesque village with a couple of tiny shops, a temple, and cows and goats that ran around freely. Several members of my family had lived here, and this was where Grandmother Baa was born. There were children who played outside and went to school for only a few hours. This was another village that had no electricity or running water, but there was a lovely river from where the women fetched the water, carrying it in big pots on their heads. I had a go at doing that myself, with great difficulty. I absolutely fell in love with this village during our week there. We stayed in my grandmother's old house, which was now owned by her nephew Hyder and family. Hyder passed away recently. We actually slept on the open balcony, where we could look up directly to the stars. It felt like being in heaven.

There was just the one television set in the village and everyone would gather around to watch. This was when the truth really hit home for me: the West may have all the materialism, but here was where the real peace was to be found. Peace was made up of things such as fresh fruit and vegetables, small houses—so little and yet so much. Back in the West, by contrast, for all our material possessions, true peace of mind remained elusive. Every morning here, we could delight at the spectacle of the sun rising; we saw this from the top of the house where we were staying. We could also see the animals being fed and children playing outside safely, without any worry about the rest of the world. My cousin Shams went back to Mumbai, but my sister and I stayed behind, travelling around in local buses to get to know more of this fabulous country. We ended up in a town called Amreli in Gujarat, where my mum's father was born. My sister and I took off to a place called Vakaner, another little town where my grandmother's brother, Uncle Pyarali and his family lived. His wife aunt Amina was very warm and hospitable towards us making us feel very at home. Whilst travelling on separate trains to a special community gathering in Hydraybad, my aunt needed to use the restroom. She asked Sultan to keep watch at the doorway, surprisingly when she exited Sultan was no longer there. No one has seen or heard from him since, this tragic disappearance left an emotional impact on my family, my aunt still waits for the moment when he will walk back in through the front door.

After this we visited a place called Rajkot, a fairly large town, where we relaxed with my grandmothers brothers, their hospitality was like nothing I had ever seen, they were waiting with garlands to welcome us to their town! My cousins, Umed, and his wife, Naseem, showed us everywhere of interest, and I ended up becoming great friends with their daughter, Habiba, and her husband whom I correspond with today.

My mum's brother, Uncle Shaukat, lived in one of the houses that had been owned by my grandfather. He was a very generous and hard-working man, and he lived there with his family. He owned an ice factory where, tragically, one of his young daughters had fallen into an ice well and died. She had slipped and fallen in, on her way from school. I learnt that when she failed to arrive home, her parents went looking for her, without success. Panic struck as the hours and minutes ticked by and the whole town eventually joined in the search. My uncle sobbed uncontrollably as he told us this story. What pain he must have suffered. How could one ever overcome such a tragedy?

As we sat down together one evening, Uncle Shaukat told me a great deal about my history and the family tree on my mum's side. Whilst subsequently writing this book, I have also learnt much family history from Uncle Amir. My great grandfather on Mum's side, Ali Bhai Devraj, was one of the richest men in Amreli, a district of the Saurashtra region of Gujarat. He married a lady called Sakina. He owned a considerable number of sugar cane factories. He was also a famous dealer in precious stones and diamonds. Although he was wealthy enough to own a Rolls Royce, his favourite form of transport was actually horse and cart! His wife, Sakina, had five sons, of whom my grandfather, Esmail, was one.

In 1903, my grandfather Esmail, went to Uganda to teach at a very young age, together with my grandmother Jena and all their children—Shirin, Laila, Kassam, and Shaukat, the youngest. My mum and uncle Amir were born in Masindi. In 1939, my grandmother decided to visit her mother, who was suffering from ill health. My grandfather, being a teacher and so heavily committed, could not accompany her back to India, so she went by herself with all the children, sailing on a ship called the *Karanja*. In those days, one had to bring one's own mattresses and sleep on the deck. The voyage took fifteen days. A few months after their arrival in India, the Second World War broke out in September 1939, and my grandmother found herself stranded in India with her family. With my grandfather still in Uganda, she somehow had to earn a living in order to provide for the children. She only knew farming, and so she ended up renting a farm called Tarvadi, where she worked endless hours to provide for her children—including my mum, who was only two years old when they arrived in India.

Grandmother Jena was a very strong woman, which was just as well given her circumstances. The war prevented any communication between Grandmother and Grandfather. There were no letters or phone calls, and she really struggled to bring up the children. Four of them eventually married, with the two boys and their wives staying with her and the girls and their husbands moving elsewhere in Gujarat.

In 1952, seven years after the war had ended, my grandfather managed to travel to India. There he arranged for my grandmother and the two unmarried children—my Uncle Amir and Mum—to return with him to Africa. In Masindi Port, my mum met my dad, and they got married. Uncle Amir married a lady called Gulshan. Many years of hard work earned my grandfather promotion to head teacher at Masindi Public School, which I was to attend in the years to come.

In 1958, my grandfather suffered the onset of chest pains but refused to see a doctor. The school term was coming to an end and he had much to do and did not want to go into the hospital, because he did not want the students' studies to be affected by his absence. There were also end-of-term exams approaching and he wanted to be there, fully committed as always. The term ended peacefully and Grandad finally decided to see the doctor because his health was deteriorating. Uncle Amir hired a taxi to take him to the hospital, accompanied by my grandma. Alas, on the way there he felt very ill and asked for some water. My grandma asked the taxi driver to stop the car. She got out to find some water, but before she returned he had stopped breathing altogether, and it was too late. Uncle Amir was only 14 years old and was too young to understand death. He tried to wake up my granddad, but Grandma covered his face with her scarf and told my uncle that he would not breathe again; he had gone to be with God. Then the shock hit her, and she burst out crying. Somehow my grandmother came to terms with her latest hardship, and in the years to come she visited India many times to see her other children. Uncle Amir had five children: Minaz, Rozy, Munira, Jangir, and Noorani. Jangir is now a doctor and Noorani is a lawyer.

The year 1959 was notable for lots of issues between Hindus and Muslims, which became very political. The Muslim farmers were targeted. There was an incident where the farmer who lived next door had killed a cow in his farm and thrown it across the fence. Then he had called out the police and filed a complaint against my Uncle Kassam for killing the cow. The cow was a sacred animal in India, and it was forbidden to kill it. The police, without listening to the truth, locked my uncle up in a cell. There was a court case filed against him, which cost him a lot of money. Luckily, my grandma was visiting India and spent all her money trying to free my innocent uncle. She even sold her jewellery to pay for the court case. My uncle eventually won his case, but atrocities like this kept on happening. For their own safety, therefore, it was only wise for Uncle Kassam's family to leave, and they were driven to Pakistan.

After their return to Masindi, Uncle Amir, Aunt Gulshan -and, their children; Minaz, Rozy, Munira, Jangir and Nooriani, and Grandma moved to Kampala, the Ugandan capital, with the children. They bought a house in Mengo, opposite Bulange House, which belonged to Kabaka. They went into the embroidery business and made beautiful saris. Shaida was studying in Kampala at the Old Kampala Secondary School and lived with my dad's sister, Roshan. Dad would visit Shaida whenever he was in Kampala to buy goods for his shop, and she would come home during the school holidays. In 1972, they left Uganda for England They were taken to a camp near Newmarket and from there they initially joined Aunt Gulshan's brother, who was already living in South Harrow. Then they moved into their house. They relaunched their embroidery business, which went on for many years. They worked extremely hard, and Grandma looked after the children and household chores.

Uncle Kassam moved to Kenya, and today his family owns Kenya Fisheries, one of the biggest firms in Kenya, employing hundreds of people. Uncle Amir moved to Kenya to help in this business for a few years, and then Uncle Shaukat followed suit with his family. It was a move that would ultimately cost Uncle Shaukat his life. Whilst working in the factory, he had an accident with a piece of metal and was fatally poisoned in the process. Uncle Kassam also died after a period of ill health, leaving my grandma devastated once more. Here was a woman who had battled all her life, someone who had endured the long separation from her husband in the war years, and then she had lost her sons, one after another. The combination of tragedies had helped reduce her to a very fragile, old lady. She was stricken with grief and clearly no longer possessed the strength and the will to do battle with any more of life's challenges. Uncle Amir took her to Kenya with him for a change of scenery, hoping it would act as a belated tonic for her. None of us realised that this would in fact be the last time we would see her. We accompanied her to the airport to wave farewell, and strangely enough, she kept looking at my mum in particular. Looking back, I suspect she had a powerful sense that this would be the last time she would see her.

Uncle Amir told us that one evening, at the end of dinner, as she was cutting some fresh mangoes to share with him, Grandma complained about a chest pain. She so rarely complained about anything, but she said the pain was becoming severe and that it was something new. He placed her on a chair near her bed, asked her to keep still, and then he called for the doctor. The doctor confirmed that she was having a massive heart attack and needed to go to the hospital immediately. Shortly after she arrived at the hospital, she passed away very peacefully. She truly deserved a quick and peaceful death. Life had been so very cruel to her, but at least her death was otherwise. She was a mightily independent person and, even in her last moments, never asked for anything. She departed this world full of humility and free of debt.

I am very tearful as I write this, not only because my grandma is no longer with us, but also because of a heightened awareness of just how blessed I have been to have had a grandma like her, and to learn so much about life as a result. The house that I live in today was first blessed by her. I have always set great store by the elderly performing that time-honoured first ceremony, to mark the new possession of a property. When our ownership papers came through, Grandma lived only a few miles away from us, so my husband Amir fetched her over to carry out the ceremonial first opening of the front door of the house. On her advice, I named this house "Bismillah," which means "in the name of God".

CHAPTER 10

Babies and Business

Initially I wanted to be a lawyer, although that's not the way things turned out! I studied at Garratt Green School in Wandsworth, I got the necessary grades in maths, biology and business studies to study law at Brunel University. But I decided to take a gap year instead and visited India, and what a fabulous trip it was. I learnt so much about life and being away from home. It really broadened my horizons. I was 19 when I returned in 1982 to my family home in Pretoria Road, Streatham. My father was very disappointed that I had not pursued my career plan, because he had put so much importance on education throughout our lives.

Three years earlier, when I was still 16, I had started a Saturday job. First I worked for K Shoes on Regent Street, which was fun. Carnaby Street was close by, and I had always loved fashion, so the scene gave me great pleasure. I would spend my entire lunch hour wandering around Regent Street and Carnaby Street. Occasionally I would walk to Bond Street. It was such a novelty in those days to walk around Bond Street and look at the glamorous windows with their lovely dresses and shoes. There was a different feel about it. Or maybe it was just that I did not have enough money to actually go into these shops and look at the designer clothes close up. Sometimes in life it can be a thrill just to look at things that are beyond reach—and then when they do finally come within reach, the novelty wears off, and it's just not quite the same somehow. Also, one learns that all that glitters is not necessarily gold! I also had a Saturday job in Harrods, which I loved. I met up with a lot of celebrities in the makeup department. During Christmas, the lights on display in the city were fabulous, especially the Harrods ones, which maintained exceptionally high standards. These jobs disciplined me a lot, especially Harrods, because they were very particular about the standard of work. I learnt quickly.

Another must was going to the theatre or the famous London Palladium. My friends and I would see a show and then go on to maybe a night club or a pop concert. I remember being a screaming teenager at a David Essex concert at the Apollo. David had 19 top-forty singles in the UK and my favourite of his songs was Rock On. Then at the end we ran behind the stage to get a glimpse of David. We stood there until the security guards threw us out. We had not a fear in the world. It was nice to be young-spirited and free. How I wish I could live those years again. It's tragic to know time cannot be wound back.

Meanwhile, for my long-term career aspirations, I decided to go into banking. I looked through the newspapers, studied the Situations Vacant, and made some phone calls. After about a month, I landed my first job in this sector. Following a series of interviews, I was taken on as a clerk by Midland Bank—"the listening bank", as it used to be known—at their branch in Tower hill, London. Why was I attracted to banking? Probably the money! If a child of mine were to take that attitude now, I would be very angry, and I guess I must have been a big disappointment in this respect to my dad, the poor man!

After about three years, I met Amir, my future husband. Our meeting came about through the Ismaili Centre in South Kensington, a focal point for community gatherings. About once or twice a year the Centre held community festival celebrations. That was how Amir and I, and our respective families met. Amir, who I subsequently learnt was manager of Barkers' Shoe Shop in Knightsbridge, came up to me at one of these events and asked me out on a date. My sister Sahera mischievously suggested that I agree to go out with him—and then stand him up! Apparently, Amir (who was one of eight children, four boys and four girls) had a reputation as something of a ladies' man. Then my grandmother made her own contribution, urging me, "Go and put some lipstick on, that boy next to you is very nice!" She was a typical grandmother, longing to see her grandchildren settled.

I did as she suggested, and when I returned from the make-up room I accepted Amir's invitation, and we arranged our date. We were supposed to meet at Tooting Broadway tube station at 6.00 p.m., but I was deliberately late—very late! I was, in fact, still at Tower Hill at 6.00 p.m., and that was an hour and a half from Tooting Broadway. I had left the bank late that day, and it was about 8.30 p.m. when I finally arrived at Tooting Broadway.

I did not expect to see Amir still standing there, waiting for me, but that was precisely what I did see, complete with a beautiful bouquet of flowers in his hands. He looked so handsome in his lovely light coloured suit. I thought, "Oh my God, he's still here. What on earth am I going to do now? How can I get out of this?" Then I thought, "Do I want to get out of this?"

Well, I could not and did not get out of it. He took me out for to dinner at Khan's Restaurant in Bayswater. He was a real charmer and behaved throughout like a true gentleman. After the meal, he took me for a walk in Hyde Park. I was quite cold with the evening chill, so he took off his jacket for me to wear, and that made me think, "Wow, he's nicer than I thought. He's a real gentleman—he's not that bad!" He took me home, opening and closing doors for me along the way. We began dating regularly, but he always had to have me back home by 10.00 p.m. That was my father's orders, and he was very much a disciplinarian. One day, alas, we got back a full hour late. We were walking up my road at eleven, and I could see Dad looking out of the window. He came outside, looked at both of us, and asked Amir, "What time do you think this is, to be bringing her home at this time of night?" Then, with the awesome significance slowly dawning on me, he added, "If you really want to be with her, you will have to sign some documents, won't you?" He was referring to marriage, wasn't he? His remark was code for, "Is it not better that you marry her? Then you can stay out together as long as you like." Amir, chirpy chap that he always was, replied, "Yes, we can go to the registry office in the morning!"

This happened after we had been dating for about six months. After we had said good night and I was back in my room, I had another "Oh my God" moments, thinking, "Indirectly, he has just proposed to me." I also recalled the grin on Dad's face during that life-changing conversation! The next day, Amir phoned his parents, asking them to come over to my house to meet mine, which they did. Two days after that late-night encounter with Dad, Amir formally proposed to me. As with so much about him, it was not entirely conventional. He simply pulled over and stopped his car on the hard shoulder as we were driving across London Bridge. He duly asked me to marry him and I said yes. He dropped me off at home, I told my parents, and they and my Sahera could scarcely contain their excitement—they almost literally jumped for joy.

It is an Indian custom to invite the boy's parents to your home for approval. A couple of days later, Maa and Bapa came to meet my parents with Amir. My mother and grandmother, with great excitement, made many dishes because they were invited to supper that evening. Both sets of parents met, and we got on very well, so we were on our way to matrimony. I often visited Amir's home in Twickenham and got to know the family very well. They were very welcoming and kind towards me. We were married in April 1985, at Wandsworth's Registry Office, and we went to live at Amir's family home in Twickenham with his parents, four brothers, and two sisters. At that stage, I was still working for the Midland Bank, although I had given up the Saturday. Amir joined the family business.

Then I gave up my bank work for the family business—the general store with the post office in Twickenham. The family lived above the shop. Amir and I did this for about three years, with him helping in the general store and me working in the post office. Our working hours were the standard 9.00 a.m. to 5.00 p.m. We then took over another family business for about a year in Basingstoke, which was run by my brother-in-law, Noore, and his wife, Laila. Noore had built this to such a high spec and enjoyed a good few years there until they emigrated to Canada. We moved back to Twickenham, and my sister-in-law, Parvis, and her husband, Anish bought the Basingstroke business.

In October 1987, I became pregnant with Farzana, my first child. I continued working until the final month of my pregnancy, and she was born at the West Middlesex Hospital. After this, Amir and I decided to go our own way. We felt we wanted to start something on our own, and so we started looking at businesses for sale in the South East with Bapa's help. Everything seemed so expensive, but then, looking through a national newspaper, our eyes set upon a little a grocery store in Ascot. We phoned its owners and discovered the business was for sale—We would lease the premises. It was in the middle of a council estate and I thought, "With all these houses, we could establish a mini-supermarket that could do really well." In those days, there were no local Tescos, no big megastores—or at least not to the extent and size that they are now.

We bought the shop with a bank loan, backed up by my father-in-law, who was kind enough to provide a guarantee. We had got to know a Lloyds Bank manager, Mr Jenkins, who was kind enough to lend us the money for working capital. Life in Ascot began with a great sense of moving forward. We moved into a little flat above the shop. It was a nice mini-market that was open from 8.00 a.m. to 6.00 p.m., Monday to Saturday. It was fairly busy, but we could see that there was room for improvement. The flat was basic in the extreme, but we managed. The most precious thing was our little baby girl, Farzana, who was just three months old. She was a very good baby. I would do the morning shift in the shop while Amir looked after her, and he would do the afternoon shift. We extended the shop's opening hours from 8.00 a.m. to 11.00 p.m., seven days a week, in order to boost our takings. With no rival supermarkets in the area, our business flourished with God's grace.

Time flew by. While I was busy in the shop, Farzana spent much of her childhood there, with lots of attention from customers. They loved her and always used to bring her gifts. Some old ladies would bring her knitted cardigans and hats and others brought along toys for her to play with. These people were amazing and I truly got to love the local community spirit. It was lovely to walk down the road or the local park where everybody knew us, or stopped to talk to Farzana. She thoroughly enjoyed being in that shop, and as she grew older and the shop got even busier, both Amir and I were required in the shop, so we decided to place Farzana in a nursery. When she was four she went to Brigidine, a convent school in Windsor. It was a lovely school on King's Road near Windsor Great Park, and the headmistress was a gentle lady named Mrs Cairns. I would see her in the corridors telling her pupils to pull their skirts down with a grin on her face. Farzana was very much a Daddy's girl, and he would take her to school at the start of the day, then I would pick her up at the end of it. She greatly enjoyed school and made friends very quickly. Some of those friends remain, even today. When Farzana was six, we decided that she needed a garden in which to play. We were lucky because one of our customers was selling their house; they were moving out of the area. We had a look at it and were very impressed by it, especially the large grounds and the four huge bedrooms.

We next contacted our bank, with which we had built up a good business relationship by now. They were willing to lend the money but needed a down payment. Even though the business was doing well, cash flow was dire because of our financial commitments such as business loan repayments, so we were unable to raise the deposit, but we did not want to let go of the house. Amir had always been brave enough to take risks—he was certainly braver than I ever was—and so he borrowed ten thousand pounds on a credit card to provide for the deposit. We decided that although the house needed some refurbishment work to make it more habitable, we would, nonetheless, move in until we could afford it.

We had a new home, but I had been feeling under the weather and went to the doctor for a check-up. I saw Dr Macmarth, a very fine man and a brilliant doctor, who unfortunately is no longer with us. He suffered a fatal heart attack, but his wife, Margret, remains a great friend of ours. Dr Macmarth told me why I was feeling under the weather: it was because I was expecting another baby! This was great news. I thought, a new house, a new baby and new company for Farzana! I looked ahead and saw myself dropping Farzana off at school and bringing the baby to work with me. This was no longer any kind of obstacle for me because I had already had the experience of bringing up Farzana in the shop from the time she was three months old. The purchase of the house had gone through, and I was so excited. However, the move from the flat was not to be. My first three-month scan showed that I was expecting twins. Now what were we going to do? A new home, two babies and the shop. Amir could not possibly run the shop by himself, he needed me there, too. We only had part-time staff for stacking shelves. It would be impossible to run the shop with two babies. We reluctantly concluded that it was better for us not to move.

Instead, Amir had the idea that we would rent out the house, which would pay for the mortgage, and then he went a step further. Because the rooms were so large, he decided to divide them, creating nine rooms altogether. Amir's old school friend and one of the nicest people I know, a real diamond named Kenny joined in this enterprise. Without his help, this would not have been possible. Amir had grown up with him, and I knew him and his family really well. His sister, Caroline, was a good friend, and his mum was a real gem. He had a lovely brother, Geoff, who was a really nice guy and had a gorgeous wife, Cynthia. Over the years we got to know the whole family, and we feel a great sense of loss now that Mum and Geoff are no longer with us. Geoff was killed in a bike accident, and Ken's mum died of cancer.

After the shop closed, Amir, Kenny, and I would go across to what we called Ascot House. The two men handled the building side and I helped with the painting, with Farzana in her pushchair. She was such a good little girl, always content and smiling. Amir would pick her up now and then, sing to her, and then put her back in the pushchair. We were blessed with this property because it represented a real breakthrough in our lives, this was how we got onto the property ladder. After the Ascot House purchase, Amir continued to expand the buy-to-let property business. We began attending auctions. We would buy run-down properties, and Amir and his team would repair them to high standards I had my monthly pregnancy check-up at Heatherwood Hospital in Ascot. My doctor, Mr Tricky, advised me to take it easy and refrain from heavy lifting, because I was carrying the twins very low. However, being stubborn by nature, I ignored the advice and carried on as normal.

I was alone in the shop one evening when my water broke. Thank God there was a buzzer in the shop by the till, which was connected to upstairs. Amir and Ken were both having supper while babysitting for Farzana. The ordeal began, I suddenly felt a little foot. That meant only one thing—I was going to drop the twins any minute now! My poor little Zahra was about to come out. Amir and Ken came rushing down and called the ambulance, and within minutes I was taken to Heatherwood, where the twins were born under C-section. They were a girl and a boy. Farzana was overjoyed that she now had a brother and a sister. The boy, Alikhan, was four pounds, and the girl, Zahra, was three pounds. They were so tiny and had to be put into incubators for the next six weeks. I was allowed to stay the first week with them, and then I went home, visiting the hospital three times a day. My twins had beautiful tiny faces, but it was so scary to see them behind that glass. Sometimes at home, I would torture myself with thoughts that they might not survive. With the grace of God, they were out of hospital within three months. There was a history of twins on my family's side, so it was very likely that one of my dad and mum's siblings would also have twins. My grandmother on Dad's side had my twin uncles, Hassan and Hussein, and I was the lucky one to continue that inheritance. I counted my blessings.

Now we definitely needed a house, because the flat had only two bedrooms, and we needed space and a garden for the three children. Then coincidence—or was it fate once more?—steered my life forward again. I had to take the twins to a clinic, and on my way back I missed a turning. As a result, I drove past a house with a For Sale board outside, so I stopped and looked at it. I fell in love with the front door, which is still the door we have today; it was a beautiful mahogany brown. As I drove into the driveway of that house, an elderly lady, Mrs Smith, came out. I asked her if she was the owner and she confirmed that she was. She invited me inside, with the twins, for a cup of tea. She showed me around and instantly fell in love with Alikhan and Zahra. The garden was the clincher. It was an amazing site. Her husband was very proud of his garden and had maintained the grounds to a very high standard until he had passed away a few years earlier. Mrs Smith wanted to move into a small bungalow around the corner, which was convenient for her.

I got to the shop and excitedly told Amir about it. I had taken the number of the estate agent and we called them straightaway. Amir made the necessary arrangements for us to view the property. This time Mrs Smith's son was there, and he was asking for a slightly higher price than Mrs Smith had quoted me, but she stressed that if we really wanted the house she would abide by the original price, because she loved the twins and felt so strongly that she wanted them to grow up there. Our offer was accepted.

We had a lovely Lloyds manager, David Morsen, with whom we got on well. He was a bit concerned that the house needed a bit of work, but he saw the potential and so agreed to lend us the money. We bought the house and moved in immediately. By this time Farzana was much older, and the twins were two. Life got easier because I put them in a nursery so that I could carry on working.

As Farzana got older, I would pick up all three children and take them home. They would have their supper, and I would then return to work. Farzana, now into her early teens, would look after them and at the same time do her homework. She took on a real motherly role to them; she would play with them and sit them down with their milk. Sometimes, because of her passion for music, she would arrange a little concert with them. I grew up in a family that had a great passion for music. My grandfather, Tejani, was a very gifted at playing the sitar, and my father could play the drums. I learnt Indian classical music with Asif Bhatti and Mohammad Kassam who were fantastic music teachers and good friends of my neighbour, so it was important to me that my children take on music as a hobby. Sometimes when I came home tired all three of them would entertain Amir and myself. This would make us incredibly happy and take away all the tiredness. Sometimes Farzana would even put the twins to bed if I was really late.

She continued her studies at the Brigidine, and I built up a great friendship with the headmistress, Mrs Stanley, a fine woman who knew how to discipline her girls. Later on Farzana became head girl, and her music talent earned her a lot of awards and a music scholarship. The twins went to the reputable St George's Windsor Castle school. It was in a fabulous location, next to Windsor Castle. The school had access to St George's Chapel in the castle and had permission to use it for concerts during Easter and Christmas services and other important occasions. I could not believe how fortunate I was to be able to send Alikhan and Zahra to such a fine school. Children studying there at the same time included Princess Eugenie, daughter of Prince Andrew. Twice we saw both Prince Andrew and Sarah Ferguson. Also, Prince Edward and Sophie Rhys Jones visited the school a few months before their wedding. The twins took in a small present for them, and they were delighted.

The teachers were fabulous, and I had a special bond with a lady called Miss Griffin, who was head of the junior department. There were other lovely teachers, such as Sharon Foster, Mrs Blythe and Mr Foran, along with Mr Jones, the headmaster, and his wife. Above all, we had lovely teachers like Mr and Mrs Cartwright, who lived in the grounds of Windsor Castle and taught music to our twins. Through the Cartwrights, Zahra met a lovely teacher, Mr Manners who was teaching music in the grounds of Windsor Castle. The Cartwrights were fantastic at teaching Farzana Music whilst she was at the Brigidine School. Mr Manners a very talented man and he taught Zahra and his three daughters various instrumental skills.

While the girls were at St George's, we met a lovely family: Naseer and Zuleikha Lakahani and their two delightful daughters, Alysia and Anoushka, who were at school there. Zuleikha saw me in the car park, and with her friendly nature, she came across and started talking to me. We have been friends ever since. Naseer would very kindly pick up the twins from school when I couldn't manage it and take them home with his children. Zuleikha would give them supper, make sure they finished their homework, and then return them to me. I don't think I would have managed without the Lakhani family. Their kindness and generosity were beyond belief. Zuleikha's mother, Zera bai, a very loving lady, was with us for many years. She had such a kind nature, but we lost our dear Zera bai a few months ago. Alysia and Anoushka did very well at school and are both at Bath University, but we still meet up during the holidays and share a great bond. I miss those great times we shared when the children were all growing up together—those sports days, the end of year balls, the school picnics, and the Christmas concerts.

We also had a very strong friendship with Chrissy and Andy, who were running the Royal Foresters Restaurant in Ascot, and we used to share the school journey with them. They have two lovely children, Amy and Sam, who have grown up now and are both working. We used to celebrate a lot of New Year's parties with them. Chrissy, like Zuleikha, was very generous and would help me out with the children if I was tied up in the shop. They would take Farzana with them to Spain on holiday and spoil her. Amy would spend a lot of time with us at home over the summer holidays. Farzana left Brigidine with A levels to study law at Brunel University. She got a degree in law and carried on for another couple of years. Today, with the grace of God, she is a qualified barrister working for a firm in London. She has a hard-working Oxford educated Greek boss, Mr Vassos, a incredible nice human being, down to earth chap, a true professional with whom she gets on well. She has learnt a lot from him and his firm Melton and Legal.

After St George's, Zahra went to the Abbey in Reading, another great school with an excellent work ethic and whose headmistress was Mrs Stanley, a person who was strict but very good at achieving the best results in the area. Zahra too has passion for music and works extremely hard at her studies. She has great musical talent: she sings, plays piano, and is a music scholar. Both Zahra and Ali were at Shiplake College in Henley, where they were taking their A Level exams in summer 2012, and both are now going to university. Zahra wants to study FRENCH law and, wishes to work for the UN. Ali on the other hand wants to study equine veterinary science; he has a passion for animals, especially horses, and has been riding from a young age. He is a very gentle soul who hates any form of cruelty inflicted on animals.

A very good friend, Zara Leanne and her mother jointly owned a horse called Magic. On many occasions I would spend afternoons with Zahra's lovely family, who were very hospitable. When Ali was about ten, I used to take him when I was visiting Zara. John, Zara's husband, kindly took Ali out on Magic, and Ali fell in love with Magic and tried to persuade me to buy him a horse. Looking after a horse was not an easy job, so I kept putting it off. Fate intervened when we lost this lovely lady Anita, Zara'a mum, through cancer. Zara decided to give Magic to Ali. It was so nice of her and John, especially when their own children, Andrew, John, Leanne, and baby John, loved Magic so much. We stabled Magic in Ascot, near our shop, and I took Ali there most evenings. He learnt how to look after a horse very well. However, as time went on, Magic began to lose weight, and we had to call in a vet. The poor animal was sick and Ali tried everything to get him well. The lady at the stables did not want a sick horse there, so without Ali's permission she drove him early one morning to the vet's surgery and left him outside.

That morning I drove around to all the stables in the area and found one that was very impressive, Brook Field run by John and Chloe, in Warfield. They are experts in their field, and I don't think there is anything about horses that they do not know. Chloe was really nice about it and stabled Magic there while the vet tried to save him for another year. Ali nurtured him with all his heart, but eventually we lost the battle and had to put Magic down. Ali was devastated. It was then Ali realised that he wanted to devote his life to saving animals. John and Chloe realised how devastated he was, so they very kindly invited him to look after their gorgeous horse Zena. She was utterly adorable. Ali began to have lessons and learnt a lot from them. They were absolutely wonderful to him. Zena needed to retire, so we bought Ali a horse called Captain—a very sweet and clever animal that he still has.

Ali now goes to ride in the great park in Windsor. He takes part in competitions and helps out at the yard in between studying. I believe it was fate that brought me to Anita, who then brought Magic to Ali, and that led to Zena and Captain. God works in mysterious ways and, believe me, the experiences I have had in life leave me convinced that He does. Ali was guided to look after Magic, and through his kindness in nurturing Magic, he ended up at John and Chloe's, where he found his true niche.

We have also been very lucky to be invited to become members of Royal Enclosure at The Ascot Race Course by our dear friends David Smalley and his lovely wife Majorie. The whole family would dress up, the ladies in their hats and fine frocks, whilst the men in their morning suits. David and Majorie would invite us every year to a picnic in the car park before we went in for the races. We usually attended on Ladies Day during the Royal Ascot Week.

The twins have been very fortunate with their schools. These have included Shiplake, a very picturesque school with wonderful grounds set on the Thames near Sonning in Henley. Ali was there from the age of thirteen and loved it. Mr Davies, the headmaster, had a very good ethic and told children, "Learn to excel in what you are best at." The atmosphere there was a very happy one. He was a very easy-going man, but he knew how to discipline the pupils. His wife was a teacher there and she was a very kind lady who was always pleasant to talk to.

As I write this book, I am very emotional because I cannot bear to think that from next year, God willing, Ali and Zahra are both going to be away from home at university. Farzana is already away except at weekends, and now I have to let go off the twins.

For so many years, I have juggled between various schools and my businesses, but I will miss all this because the twins will take away a big chunk of me with them. But as parents we have to let go. They are children only for a little while; they grow up and begin to fly, and we have to let them do that.

Back in the world of work, meanwhile, Amir has built a sizeable property portfolio and oversees maintenance work and personally carries out some repair work. He now spends just two hours or so in the shop each week. For my part, I had always been a very keen traveller, and that is where my own next business venture lay. The travel industry looks glamorous, but it's not really, as I found out! I read in a newspaper that the Global Travel Group were selling franchises, so in 2006 I bought one and set up Jamie's Travel, which I ran from the office at the back of the shop. I thought, "What better location for my new venture than inside my own shop, where so many people know me already?" First, of course, I had to learn the trade via weekend courses in Chester and home study, but at the end of it all, including exams, I became a qualified travel agent! Amir also studied and qualified. Jamie's Travel was largely me, with a little help from Amir, and that's the way it has stayed. It got off to an encouraging start and business was good in the early days. Inevitably, it suffered badly with my illness, and I lost a lot of clients. I never put a "Closed" sign up; the business just didn't operate for that period, and in such a close community, everyone simply knew that "Jamie is ill". I have since been able to rebuild the business to a large extent. And, as per the original intention, there has certainly been no shortage of travel for me as a result of my participation in this industry. I have had half a dozen immensely enjoyable trips to the Caribbean, along with visits to Spain and Italy, amongst other countries. I may yet expand Jamie's Travel—certainly, there is the physical space potential for it within the shop.

Alikhan riding CAPTAIN

Zahra Govani

Amir Govani Family.
Alikhan, Jamie, Amir, Farzana, Zahra.

Chapter 11

My Lady of Destiny

Looking back, I see that at 24 I was still very young when we moved to Ascot, and I would describe myself then as a very vulnerable young woman who wanted everything in life, as one does when one is still young. Materialism still ruled. In the near future, I could see myself with a lovely car and a nice home. With the grace of God, I already had Farzana, but I wanted a couple more children, and I wanted to live happily ever after.

At that young age, one simply does not realise that materialism and all the "good things" are not what life is ultimately all about. Realisation dawns later on that all that shines is not gold. With age comes wisdom and one grasps that peace of mind—inner contentment—is so much more important. One does have to work hard, but exposure to the spiritual side of life is equally important. That saying about getting out of life what you put into it is so true. Life really does only give you what you put into it, no more and no less.

However, it's not that easy. Hard work pays off, but a fundamental belief in yourself also helps. Through the grace of God, I have been blessed in so many ways, first with good grandparents and then with good parents, who provided the moral foundation to help Amir and me bring up our own children.

There are still times in life when one can feel very alone—lost, even. The hours that I used to cover in the shop seemed to be absolutely endless. Although I had a lot of faith in the ultimate power, I wanted to find out what life had in store for me. In my childhood, I had visited fortune tellers who would read my palm and tell me things. I would never tell my parents that I had done anything like this, because they had always taught me to leave destiny alone—I should just accept that everything was in God's hands.

One day, when it was quiet in the shop, I was browsing through a newspaper when I saw an advert promoting the services of a psychic. I was fascinated by the unknown, and so I phoned the number and spoke to a lady called Helen. She was very polite, and I accepted the first available appointment, in two days time. She gave me her address, which was on London Road, Sunningdale, not far from Ascot. I mentioned that I had a nine-month-old baby who I had to bring with me, but Helen was really nice about that and said it was fine to bring Farzana with me.

I was really excited now. Although I had been brought up to leave everything in God's hands and to have faith, I was a very daring character and wanted to know what the future held in store for me. On arrival for my first session with Helen, I realised that her house was on a very busy road, but there was a restaurant across that road where I could park the car. I got out, put Farzana in the buggy, and crossed the road. As I approached the house, this charming lady came out to greet us. Helen brought her lovely little dog, Rosie, and Farzana was overjoyed because she loved dogs. I saw a big pond in the garden where Helen kept some fish. She also had a cat.

The main house was on the left, but on the right was an outhouse, and this is where she invited us to go and sit. Again she stressed that it was okay for Farzana to be with us in there, and after a few minutes Helen brought me a lovely cup of tea. The session began and Helen borrowed my ring and held it for a little while, looking first at the ring and then at me as she spoke.

I simply could not believe how accurate she was in the things she said about me. The session lasted about an hour. As well as stunning me with the accuracy of her description, I could also see that she was really kind and very good to Farzana. She invited us into the main house and gave Farzana a glass of milk. Helen also introduced me to her friend Wyn, a very nice gentleman.

Helen, I learnt, was an Austrian who had been in England for many years and also spoke German. She impressed me as a very learned and wise lady. She also went to the Sacred Heart Church every day to help out there. She had a little section in the church where she hung Padre

Pio's picture and lit a candle there. (Padre Pio was born in Italy and became a saint.)

I never realised it at the time, but that advert in the local newspaper was the first step in the creation of a great and long-lasting friendship. It almost seemed as though I had been guided. Not only did I benefit, but Helen also became a sort of second aunt to Farzana.

Helen even helped with the business of moving home. In my anxiety to move out of the flat, I made an offer for a house that was up for sale just across the road—but Helen advised me not to go for it because there was a better house waiting for me. She actually described the house that I was going to end up buying. She gave me a very clear mental picture of a brown mahogany door, which was indeed part of the house I bought.

I worked really long hours, and with a demanding little child to look after, there were times when I felt desperately tired and even fed up. I would take Farzana with me and visit Helen and Wyn. We would sometimes take Farzana for a walk. Opposite her house there was a pathway leading to a very serene part of Sunningdale where there was a beautiful big house that belonged to the Sultan of Brunei, surrounded by bodyguards. Farther up from there, a little while away, was the house where Edward VIII with Mrs Simpson. I had read about English history and the monarchy and was really excited to be standing in front of this house. Time passed and my family grew with the arrival of the twins. During my pregnancy, I would visit Helen and ask her countless questions about the birth, but she was a true friend and never complained. Amongst her replies to my questions, she told me that she could see both blue and pink, meaning that one of the babies would be a girl and the other a boy.

As Ali and Zahra grew up, I would encourage them to learn some carols in German, and we would visit Helen on Christmas Eve. The children would light up the place by singing these carols. Both Farzana and Zahra had taken up music at school and had learnt to play the piano. Many times they performed at St George's Chapel, and twice they sang for the Queen. There was a charity concert at St Paul's Cathedral in London, in aid of blind children. Prince Charles was present, and they both had the opportunity to sing. As all mums do, I tried to put them up for everything that involved education. Helen has two boys who are both doctors and practise abroad. They visit her a lot and she often visits Austria.

Meanwhile, Wyn wanted to move back to his native Wales. Helen invited us all around to her home one evening and broke the news to us—they were going to move to Wales. This shook me, I had come to know and like her so much. But I accepted, of course, that she had a life of her own to think about and needed to move on with Wyn. She sold the house in Sunningdale and moved to Llanelli in Wales. We are still in touch and phone each other regularly. She is very fond of Farzana, Ali, and Zahra, and always sends them gifts and likes to learn of their progress.

I believe I was destined to meet Helen because, although I have my faith and she has hers, she came into my life at a time when I needed someone who could advise me about the children's education and our businesses, and that person needed to be someone I could trust, which Helen certainly was. Helen and Wyn were always there for us whenever we needed them, and to some extent they still are, although obviously the distance involved is much greater now. They are truly missed by us all, and they will always remain very dear to us.

Chapter 12

Good-bye, Dad. We All Loved You, Our Pilot, So Much

Shaida, Sahera, and I felt terrible when we phoned home from Canada and learnt that Dad was still in low spirits. We had stayed on because we had planned to go to Edmonton to see Uncle Fidai, who was also very ill at that time. Mum told us that Dad had not felt very well on the flight and had found it a very long and taxing trip on his own. We felt that if only we could have turned the clock back, one of us would have gone with him, but at the time, we just didn't think about it.

When we did eventually return to England, we found Dad still in poor condition. He had lost weight and his behaviour had changed. He would sit down on the sofa at night and fall asleep. He would put his keys somewhere and then forget where he had left them. Ferride and Pam sent him for some blood tests. He was very stubborn, and I think he had hardly ever visited a doctor in his entire life. With the grace of God, he had always enjoyed good health. Even when he had flu, he would just set about working it off and would not succumb.

His blood test revealed a lack of white blood cells, and because he had become so weak, he had to be admitted to the hospital. I remember the scene so well. Mum and all the brothers and sisters got together by the front door of our house, and my sister Shaida, brother-in-law Nizam, and my mother were going with him. He turned around and looked at us all, and then he said, "You are all forcing me to go; I never like hospitals, and I might not be back." As we were to realise later on, this was no casual remark. It was very much a message from the depths of his heart. He had known that he was suffering from cancer but had not told us. As was so typical of him, until the very last minute he was concerned with not causing us any worry; he wanted to cope with it himself.

Strangely, the night before his departure, he had locked himself in the toilet downstairs by accident. He phoned Amir to come over and repair the lock so that Mum would not get locked inside as he had done; he was evidently very aware that he might not be around for much longer because of the terminal cancer, and so he wanted it repaired as soon as possible. Dad even had his own tools in the garage for an emergency.

The news got worse with the discovery, just a day after Dad was admitted into hospital, that his cancer had spread. He had been brought back to his room after an X-ray and blood test, and he kept saying he wanted to go home. We kept convincing him that it was only a few days before he could do that and that as soon as his condition had improved, we would take him home. All the family members had gone to the Jamak Khanna for prayers, but Mum and I stayed behind.

As we were sitting by his side, talking to him, a young lady doctor came in and spoke to him. She asked how he felt, and he replied, "I am well and need to go home." The doctor then asked Mum and me to follow her into her office. We both walked in and stood there. She said, very politely, that we should sit down before she said what she had to say. Alarm bells began to ring in my head; my gut churned and I sensed all too strongly that what she was about to say to us was not good news.

She looked at Mum and calmly told her that Dad had terminal cancer, and that it was only a matter of a few weeks before we would lose him. He had lung cancer, and the cells had spread to his brain. Mum burst out crying, and I just stood there, struck dumb and numb. I had no idea what to say. It was more than I could take, more than I could deal with at that moment. Here was a man who had played such a big part in our lives. He was life itself—my dear father, whom I had always regarded as our protector—and now we were going to have to face up to the reality of losing him.

How could this be? It was too painful for words, and it was even more painful to look at Mum, who was going to be deprived of her life partner, the man she loved and had been with from the age of fourteen. The doctor was very kind and allowed us to sit with her for a little while. We then went back to Dad's room. He asked us what the doctor had said, and Mum replied, "Nothing much, only that you need to stay in hospital for now, and you will get better soon." He had a smirk on his face that told me that he was well aware of the truth. That smirk said, "I know full well that I am terminally ill, and that you are trying to fool me." No wonder he wanted so much to go home. He knew he was fast approaching the end of his life, and that was where he wanted to spend his final days.

After a long battle, Shaida and Ferride convinced Dad to undergo radiotherapy. Shaida always played a very big role in our lives, along with her husband Nizam, who never stopped her from doing anything for the family—something that we recall and respect more than ever, on reflection. Shaida kept taking time off work. They ran a garage and, by the grace of God, it was always busy. She would arrive at the hospital very early and fetch all the things that Mum needed. She was also very brave to go in the ambulance from St George's Hospital to May Day Hospital for Dad's radiotherapy sessions twice a week. He found that tough; the side effects were not pleasant. Shaida provided great comfort for both Mum and Dad throughout the ordeal.

We visited him in hospital every day. All the grandchildren would do so in the evening. Mum stayed there overnight and slept on the sofa bed. All the family members flew over from Canada, and hundreds of other people who knew and loved Dad paid a visit to the hospital. He remained very dignified and humble throughout his awful illness. He never argued about his medication or food, always eating whatever he was given. He adored his grandchildren, and one could see him glowing when they visited him one by one in the evenings.

Dad spoke very openly about his illness and displayed no fear of death. Right up until the end, he would be asking the children about their studies. Nabilla, Shaida's daughter, had gone to Cuba for a few days with her husband, Jan, and when they visited him on their return, they jokingly asked him, "What would you have liked from Cuba?" He said he wanted cigars from Havana. They actually had some, but they could do no more than show these to him because he was no longer allowed to smoke.

So many memories flooded back. In his younger days, as well as cigars, Dad had been particularly fond of good clothes and shoes.

Mum and Dad both belonged to the Lions Club when we lived in Masindi, and he used to love dancing. The functions were sometimes held at Chobe Lodge for a whole weekend. My parents would take us there; they would attend the dinner and the dances, and we would be entertained with the children's club.

One morning at the hospital, the doctor asked us if we wanted to take Dad home. We were longing for this opportunity because he kept saying this was what he wanted. Mum, Shaida, and Uncle Akbar arranged to take him home. They organised a bed in the front room because he would not have been able to climb the stairs. He came home, but as he saw that bed in the front room, he could not hide his great disappointment. He so wanted to go upstairs, but he simply couldn't manage that.

That evening he had breathing difficulties and he had to be rushed back into hospital again. The following day we found him looking really well, so our spirits soared and we felt he was going to improve once more. We just could not give up hope and prayed for a miracle. Alas, it was not to be. We left him smiling and happy, in a good mood and laughing. Mum, as usual, spent the night there. On the way home, I told Amir how happy I was to see my dad looking so good. I even said that the next day I would have a lie-in because I could relax that night with not too much to worry about. I really thought a miracle had happened and that my dear dad was going to get better. That mood shattered when, just as we got home and into bed, the peace was disturbed by the sound of the phone ringing. Amir answered and it was Nizam calling. He said that it "was time" and that we should return to the hospital as soon as we could. We got dressed quickly and went back.

On the way there, I kept praying that he would be okay. I could not bear the thought of losing him. We arrived there within 45 minutes and ran upstairs to his room. He was lucky that he had a private room. The whole family stood around him in total silence—one could have heard the proverbial pin drop. Dad was moving his head slowly from left to right, and his eyes were shut. The nurse then came in and told us that it was only a matter of a few minutes before the inevitable happened. We began to pray loudly, "Please God, make his journey as smooth as possible to the other side." No one cried. Mum stroked his head. Uncle Hadi stood by his head. Then Ferride and Pam arrived and they joined us in prayer; we could sense that Dad had been waiting for them. Shaida bravely guided Dad in his final moments. She told him, "Mum and all your family are giving you permission to go peacefully; we will all look after each other, don't worry. Mum will be all right, and we also have Uncle Hadi to look after us." Shaida asked him to recite the "Kalma," which was recited at the point of death for anyone under the Muslim faith. These were indeed his very last words, and seconds later he stopped breathing. That was when the reality hit home, and we all realised that Dad had gone. We all burst into tears. This man, who had been the pilot of the Karsan family for so long, was no longer. Just as an aircraft cannot fly without a pilot, so our family, in all its constituent parts and circumstances, could not have achieved all it had done, reached where it was today, without his guidance, leadership, wisdom, and love.

Dad's funeral was very special, with hundreds of people attending, including relatives from Canada. He is buried at the Brookwood Cemetery near Woking, Surrey, not far from where I live. I often visit the cemetery and sometimes take the children with me. We had so many letters from people telling us how Dad had helped them in all sorts of ways. We had not even been aware of some of the things he did. He had been a very charitable person, and as is so often the case with people who truly and selflessly do good in this life, he had not talked about all of it. We were so blessed to have had such a father I often visit the cemetery. I love solitude, and it might sound morbid, but I find a lot of peace in graveyards, where I can remain quiet, think about life, and let the world go by. When I am sad, I often go sit by Dad's grave and think about what he has taught us, and it's such an inspiration.

Beloved 'big man' will be sorely missed by family and customers

A prominent Asian businessman and devout Ismaili Muslim, Amirali Popat Karsan, has died of cancer, aged 71.

Originally from Uganda, Mr Karsan was well-known and highly regarded throughout Tooting, and previously Balham, where for many years he owned shops.

Until his retirement a few years ago Mr Karsan spent 14 years running the sub post office and Karson's general store in Mitcham Lane. Before that he owned a grocers in Chestnut Grove, Balham.

Before coming to the UK he ran several businesses and served as a local councillor in his native town of Masindi.

However, in 1972, he was forced to start a new life in Britain when the late dictator Idi Amin gave all of Uganda's 50,000 Asians just 90 days to leave.

In 1973 he found his way to Balham and opened his first grocery store, called Rafiki, meaning friend, as he was often referred to in Uganda.

But to his extensive family, and especially his grandchildren, he was always known as Mbwana Mkubwa, Swahili for big man.

Mr Karsan's younger brother Hussein said: "He was kind, considerate, helpful and made an impact on people who came across him. He loved reading, playing Indian drums and watching Indian soaps on Asian TV channels."

Family friend Burt Luthers said: "He was a very nice man. He did a lot of work in the community and was very popular."

Amirali Carson leaves his widow Roshanbanu, a son, five daughters and several grandchildren.

Chapter 13

Once More, a Life-Changing Turn of Events

One never knows what life has in store. I had always thought that I would work extremely hard for a number of years, and then, once our children had gone off to university, Amir and I would sell some of the properties and at long last begin to take life a little more easily. We had worked so hard for so long, and I felt—or rather I knew—that we could not keep up that pace forever. We were not getting any younger, and we were starting to feel the strain.

Neither of us had ever been the sort who could imagine completely retiring, but my own long-term aim had always been to work with a charity so that I could help those who were less fortunate then myself. God had always been very generous to me, and it was only right for me to put something back into the universe. Also, my parents had always taught me that the giving hand always counted for so much more than the receiving hand.

Alas, that quieter life and my greater giving were not to be, following an alarming and life-changing turn of events. It all began in March of 2010, shortly before we were due to fly out to Vancouver, Canada, for the wedding of my cousin, Sajid. One night, as I got off the bed to turn off the television, I suddenly felt very giddy and had a fall. I must have been knocked out for a few minutes, but I eventually regained consciousness and climbed back onto my feet, feeling a bit better as I did so. Rightly or wrongly, I returned to bed without waking up Amir, who had slept through it all. By the following morning, as a result of the fall, a big bruise had formed on my thigh, but I didn't take much notice of it at first. I chose to ignore it, believing that it would go away in a few days. Also, because of the imminent wedding, there was still so much to do, and the last thing I needed was to be flapping around over a fresh worry.

Next weekend, however, I had a visit from my pharmacist brother, Ferride. The weather was good, and so we were walking around in shorts. He couldn't help noticing my bruise. He was clearly very concerned and advised me to see a doctor for a blood test before flying, so that was my priority on Monday morning. It was really strange because I had not been to a doctor since the birth of my twins. We had been under the care of a lovely GP, Dr Macmarth, and both he and his charming wife, Margaret, took care of the family. Unfortunately, we had lost Dr Macmarth through a heart attack a few years back, and so when I went to the surgery, I saw Dr Fanning, who was absolutely brilliant. He immediately wrote me a letter to have a blood test done at Heatherwood Hospital. I returned home from the doctor and thought nothing more of it. I did in fact say to Dr Fanning that nothing much wrong would be found with me, and I would phone in for the results when I had come back after the wedding in Canada. The following day I was all set to drop the children off to school when I took a phone call from the hospital, asking me to drop everything and come in to see Dr Fanning again just as soon as possible.

I got home and was rushed to the hospital by Amir. There Dr Fanning told me that the haemoglobin was very low in my blood, and I needed a blood transfusion. I did not realise how serious this was. I wanted to ignore it because I was so anxious to be at Sajid's wedding, but Dr Fanning insisted that I should not fly. I was very fortunate to have BUPA cover, so I was urgently taken into Princess Margret Hospital in Windsor, where I saw Dr Sarsam. He was such a gentle soul—a fabulous and brilliant doctor who made room straightaway for a blood transfusion. I was not aware of the procedure and how many hours it would take, so even at this stage I was under the impression that I would get well soon enough and still fly out to the wedding by the weekend.

My recovery after the blood transfusion was slow. I felt breathless, tired, and lethargic. Dr Sarsam advised me not to fly and said he needed to perform a colonoscopy and an andioscopy. He performed these procedures on me on Wednesday and asked me to make an appointment with him for a week later to check on the results. While he carried out the procedures, he had taken out swabs, which he sent off for biopsy. A couple of days went by. I was feeling really rough now—and much worse was to follow. I got a phone call from Dr Sarsam's nurse for an emergency appointment to see him. This was when bells started to ring, and it sank in that I was not at all well. Amir and I sat down with Dr Sarsam, who asked me how I was feeling. I said I was rough but not very ill. He took out the pictures from the scopes. He showed them to me and asked me if I had any inkling as to what was happening to me. I immediately asked him if it was serious, and he replied, "Yes." He explained that the swabs he had sent for biopsy showed cancer of the bowel. On the plus side, it could be treated and removed with surgery. He said I urgently needed a CT scan to make sure that it had not spread anywhere else; he arranged this for the following day. I made some sort of weak joke and began to talk about my hair and what the cancer treatment would do to it. Dr Sarsam then explained that if that was the case, I could have a wig fitted.

As I came out of hospital with Amir, I sat down on the wall outside, totally oblivious to the traffic and the people passing by. I felt as though my whole world was crumbling before my eyes. So many questions invaded my mind. What was going to happen to my children if anything was to happen to me? I knew Amir was there, but children really needed their mother. This was the same hospital I used to pass by every day, from the time Farzana was a child to the days when I would give so many of my customers a lift here. When they used to break the news to me about being diagnosed with cancer, I used to feel so bad for them; now it was my turn to go through it. I had to lie to Mum and family. I told them that the reason I had not seen them as frequently as I normally would have done was that I had been very busy in the shop, chiefly on account of staff absences, and so I had been tied to the business more than usual. It was clear that they were not happy with this explanation, but Amir managed to keep them at bay.

I found great comfort in my lovely little shop. It always felt like a sacred haven, so I asked Amir to take me back there. I sat down at my desk and tried to come to terms with everything. Then I picked up the phone to call my brother-in-law, Nizam, who had lost his dad through cancer. When he heard my news, he was silent for a minute. Then he began to share his experience of his dad's illness and tried to convince me that the medical world had moved on a great deal since his father's time, and that my operation would be fine. Nizam advised me to keep things quiet on this side of the Atlantic. I had convinced Mum and my sisters to go to the wedding without me, pretending that I had no staff in the shop. Also, because they were already in Canada enjoying the wedding, it was only fair that they did not find out the truth about my illness until they all came back. Amir phoned his brother-in-law, Shamsher, and sister, Nilufa, who were also shocked to hear the news. Amir at this point was tearful and had to regain his composure.

I had my CT scan done on the Monday. The result proved that luckily the cancer had not extended to the lymph nodes, but I still needed the surgery. I phoned my brother and sister-in-law and told them. They were pharmacists, and so it was a big help for me to have them visit and explain everything as best they could. Mum and my sisters arrived a few days later from the wedding. I had tremendous support and care from both sides of the family and the Reading Jamat who were absolutely fabulous. My children also gave me a lot of strength. With superhuman effort, they managed to act commendably normally and kept reassuring me that all would be well. I had hundreds of cards and lovely flowers delivered to my house every day, wishing me well.

Dr Sarsam recommended Dr Desai at Wrexham, who was a specialist in colon cancer. He was another fine consultant, very softly spoken and of a very kind nature. I also had another superb doctor, Dr Frenandes who was the anaesthetist, and he had a terrific sense of humour. While he was injecting me in the spine, which was horrendously painful, he would make a funny comment to distract me from the agony. I was very frightened because I was measured up for a colostomy. I was operated on for eight hours, and when I eventually woke up, Dr Desai said that the operation had been successful and that there was no need for a colostomy. What a relief that was. At that moment, I simply could not thank God enough; my feelings of gratitude and relief were immense. When I woke up, I saw Shaida, Amir, and my children waiting around me with tears of joy.

I had a lot of visitors in hospital, so time passed by relatively quickly. I came home after a couple of weeks and was looked after by Shaida and Amir's sister, Nilufa. As I write this now, it's been over a year since that operation, and thank God, things are not so bad. Most of the time, I manage to remain positive. I believe in destiny—What will be, will be. We are all on this earth for a purpose, and trials and tribulations are a part of life.

Chapter 14

Amir's Magnificent Surprise for Me

There was something odd about the telephone conversation Amir was having at his end of our office, about twenty feet away from me. I didn't need a sixth sense to know that he was up to something. It was a June afternoon in 2011, but the beautiful British weather was momentarily forgotten as I picked up paperwork for Nairobi, Kampala, and Virgin flights. I asked him who these flights were for, and he casually replied, "Oh, just a client, don't worry about it." I guess he figured that would sound plausible enough, given that he routinely got involved in my travel agency business when I was not around.

Then I heard him talking about the Serena, which was a top hotel in Kampala. It was known as the "pearl of Africa", and it truly was a magnificent hotel. At this point, a very loud bell in my head began ringing! It got even louder when Amir went outside the office at the start of another call, which included more references to the Serena, and this time he made the call on his mobile phone! I kept quiet for a while; not letting on that I knew all was not what it appeared to be. It came out into the open that evening when, with me at his side, Amir asked our children, "I'm thinking of going away for a while with your mum. Will you be all right on your own?" As children do, they needed no encouragement. Parents away? Yes! We could do and go where we liked. And then they asked where he was taking me. Amir looked me in the eye and declared, "I am taking you to Uganda."

I felt a surge of excitement and quickly became very emotional, but I also had an immediate concern. "How can I fly?" I asked, remembering that I was not supposed to fly for up to a year after major surgery—and my operation was certainly in that category. But Amir replied reassuringly, "That can be sorted—see your doctor tomorrow." The next day I found myself in Dr Fanning's surgery and I told him what was going on and expressed my concerns about the potential implications in the wake of my operation, but he merely asked, "Are you healthy?"

"Yes," I said.

"And are you eating well?"

"Yes."

"No other problems of any kind?"

"No."

"Then I think you should be okay. Just take care what you eat and drink—don't eat at the roadside facilities, for instance." I had total faith in Dr Fanning.

So that was it, and I had the green light. My trip was definitely on. I was on a high! My visit to the doctor was on Friday, and we were flying out on Tuesday. How would we cope? Who would mind the shop? I need not have worried. Farzana, now 22, was an absolute brick. She supervised the minimarket and travel agency, and she also did a great job of looking after the twins.

Preparations for a ten-day vacation in Uganda went ahead at a furious pace. But then again, such a challenge was really nothing new or insurmountable—after all, there had been 15 years when we had run that minimarket, Amir and me, for seven days a week! I had to have my hair done, I had to have my nails done, and I always over-packed when I was going away. I took what seemed like everything with me. I don't know why I do that—I never wear half the things I take! It's just me. I phoned around all my family, telling them what we were doing. In those few, hectic days, I kept thinking, especially at night, "I wonder how those buildings from my childhood will look now? I must visit my grandfather's grave." I was going back for the first time in almost 40 years. So many thoughts raced through my head; so many emotions gripped me. Of course there had been many times when I had thought about doing this, but we were always so busy, both with our businesses and with the little matter of raising three children, and so such ambitions were always put to one side.

The great day was upon us quickly enough, and on the Tuesday evening I found myself boarding a Virgin airlines jumbo jet at Heathrow Airport—but only after another mini-drama. On attempting to check in, it became apparent that we were victims of the "bumping up" procedure, which I knew all about as a travel agent. This is the practice of deliberately over-booking a flight to take account of the inevitable late cancellations—except that on this occasion there had not been any, or at least not enough to preserve our own places.

We both protested vigorously. No doubt we would have been put up in an hotel and re-booked on another flight one or two days later—but that would have meant losing one or two days of my precious time in Uganda, and I was in no mood to accept that. They offered to upgrade us for an extra five hundred, but we did not see why we should have to pay that. Eventually, we made it into first class!

Everything had been so last minute that we had no clear plan, no pre-arranged itinerary, for our time in Uganda. We had been too preoccupied in the interim with sorting out our respective businesses, working well into every night. We discussed our itinerary on the flight out. The Virgin flight to Nairobi, Kenya, took eight hours. We had a ten-hour stopover and Amir's cousin, Jalalu, joined us to say hello. He very kindly took us to his house and also showed us around the city. His mum, whom we called Masi, had bought all types of tropical fruits for us to eat, and we were fascinated to see them after such a long time. Certain fruits are only found in the African climate. We had a great day in Nairobi meeting the rest of extended family.

At 7.00 p.m. that day, we were back to the airport, and this time we boarded a much smaller Kenya Airways plane for the short hop of one and a half hours to Kampala's Entebbe Airport. My God, I thought yet again. This really is it. I really am going back home. I was sobbing as we touched down, but I looked to Amir and managed to say, "Thank you so much for doing this." I was so excited. I thought to myself, I have truly made my dream come true.

Chapter 15

Bridging That Forty-Year Gap

We were met at the airport by my brother-in-law, Amin, his gorgeous son, Adam, and my sister-in-law, Lucy, who was also visiting Uganda. Amin's young lady, Sian, and his two lovely children, Nika and Amar, had stayed behind in England. There was wonderful warmth in the air, and my heart was bursting with joy. Not only was I visiting Uganda for the first time in 40 years—which had been an ambition so dear to my heart for so long—but I had actually achieved this ambition after overcoming the extra hurdle of my cancer scare.

I noticed that there were now two terminals at this airport; there had been just the one when I had left as a child. They had built a new one, which was much bigger and positively palatial by comparison, like something out of Dubai. The original terminal had been characterised by old and broken tiles and windows. The new one was a breathtaking marble affair. When we left in 1972, the airport staff was downright rude and rough, not to mention positively hostile, towards us. Now the contrast could not have been more complete, as we were welcomed back with great warmth and courtesy. All the memories of how we were treated at the airport when we were expelled came back with a vengeance. I could picture my poor mum, my brother and sisters, and the other Asians struggling to come to terms with what was happening to them. The air was full of gloom and doom with suffering then, and now it felt that the airport was unrecognisable, with no more fear from Amin's soldiers.

As we left the airport, I could see, in the near distance, a beautiful building all in white, which looked like a palace. I asked Amin what it was, and he said it was the state home where Musevini, the Ugandan president, resided. I remember in Idi Amin's days being driven past the Command Post, which was his home. One could not even dare to stop and look, or else one would face being arrested and sent to Makindye Jail, one of the prisons near Kampala, where torture and the killing of innocent people took place. Driving past Makindye one could see trails of blood leading from the road—innocent civilians were battered by the soldiers on the way to the prison.

It was very dark as we hit the side roads, so we could not really see very much. Amin took the turning off to Jinja Road, which led to the town of Satta, where he lived. This was about an hour's drive from Kampala. I remembered Jinja Road very well because of the Coca-Cola plant—it was still there and looked the same. The roads were a lot better than I could remember from my last time in Uganda. We entered another side road, and this one was muddy and ran between beautiful banana plantations. By now I was feeling as though I was in paradise.

At the end of this journey, we were greeted by two of my other sisters-in-law, Naseem and Parvis, who were also visiting Uganda. We were very tired by now because we had already had a stopover in Nairobi for a few hours, with Amir's cousin Jalalu and aunt Roshan feeding us so well that we were fit to burst. They had both gone the extra mile to prepare everything for the few hours we were in Nairobi.

Amin's lovely house was surrounded by beautiful scenery, as I saw when I got up the next day. I had gone to bed around 2.00 a.m. and was woken up by the birds early in the morning. With everyone else in the household still asleep, I went outside and sat on the swing in the veranda. It was amazing. I could smell the red, fertile soil. In fact, this was a smell that was quickly returning to me after so many years. Uganda had a distinctive scent, one I remembered so well from my childhood. We used to have so much fun playing with that soil, mixing it with water and creating little figurines.

It was around 7.00 a.m. and I marvelled at the beautiful early morning sunshine, the clear air, and the enveloping warmth. The temperature was already up to around 25 degrees, and it would rise to 30 at midday, albeit with a tempering breeze. I could see countless birds, and papaya trees with ripe fruit in the garden next door. What a different world this was from the one I inhabited now. I reflected how the West might have everything in the materialistic sense, yet it could never match this country for peace of mind. It was all so far away and yet so near—Uganda was just eight hours away on a flight, which was not really a lot, it seemed. I actually pinched myself to make sure that I was not dreaming all this.

I was out there for an hour observing nature. In the near distance, I could see the men and women already at work with their farming tools, the women with their babies tied to their backs as they prepared to plough the fields. They looked so strong, and I suspected most of them had never heard of babysitters. They would scarcely have had enough money to feed themselves adequately, let alone afford to pay for such luxury extras as child-care services. A lot of the Ugandans grew their own crops, such as bananas, cassava, sweet potato and millet. Sometimes the temperatures were soaring, and still men and women ploughed the fields in order to provide food for their families. Even with such hardships, one could see a lot of happiness amongst them—they were so full of life and love for each other. As for me, I just sat there on that swing thinking, "This is my Uganda. I am here—yes, I am really here". This was a moment in a million, and my heart was bursting with excitement.

On that first day, after breakfast, Amin took us around Kampala. The city is divided into five boroughs, of which Kampala district was one. Initially, Mutesa I, the Kabaka (king) of Buganda, had chosen the area of Kampala, which was then made up of hills and wetlands, to be one of his hunting grounds. The city grew on a large scale after the severe damage of the war between Uganda and Tanzania. Kampala was rebuilt with new hotels, banks, hospitals, schools, and a fundamental improvement of the infrastructure. Kampala is a city built on seven hills—including Kasubi Hill and Mengo Hill, which is the headquarters of the Buganda Court of Justice and also has the Kabaka Palace or Lubiri of Baganda and the Buganda Parliament, known as Lukiko. Strangely enough, Grandma Jena used to live opposite the Lukiko, so I was used to seeing soldiers with guns guarding the place.

The third hill is the Kibuli, which has the famous Kibuli Mosque. As we drove through Kampala, we could see this magnificent white mosque, and I could remember it so vividly, just as I had seen it in my childhood. I could not believe that it still looked exactly the same. The fourth hill is the Namirembe, home to the Anglican Cathedral. The fifth is the Lubaga Hill, with the Rubaga Catholic Cathedral. The sixth,

Nsambya Hill, now houses Nsambya Hospital. The seventh is Kampala Hill, where construction of a mosque was begun by Idi Amin but never completed. Kampala has other smaller hills, such as the Nakasero, which is one of the upmarket areas, where some of the five star hotels are located. The Mulago Hill has the namesake hospital—the largest hospital in Uganda. When Aunt Begum was suffering from breathing difficulties because she had a hole in her heart, she was treated there under a very clever doctor by the name of Dr K. M. Patel.

I was really impressed with Kampala, although the volume of traffic was double to what it had been when I was a child. There were cars everywhere now. What really took me by surprise was that the Ugandans and the Asians were trading side by side; to see this brought a great joy to my heart. Great changes had taken place for the better, and I longed to see more. Indeed, Uganda had moved on in so many ways. It gave me great pleasure to see that the local people owned their businesses and that there was such a huge growth in the economy. Britain had granted Uganda independence on 9th October 1962, and Dr Milton Obote became the first Prime Minister of independent Uganda. Uganda became a republic in 1963 and Kabaka Mutesa II became a President, but real power was transferred to the Prime Minister. This led to the removal of the traditional kingdoms. Today President Musevini, is both head of state and head of the government. He has been re-elected several times and has brought great changes to the economy and reduced poverty considerably. He has been very kind to invite the Asians back to Uganda.

We thoroughly enjoyed that tour of Kampala, courtesy of Amin. He showed us the sights, including the Aga Khan School where my uncles, Hassan and Hussein, had studied, and the Old Kampala School attended by my eldest sister, Shaida. Amin also took us to Makerere University and Mulago hospital, where my aunt Begum was treated before she went to India for her surgery. Amin then drove us to Mengo to see the house where Grandma Jena had lived, opposite the Lukiko. We also saw the nearby Ismaili Centre on Namirembe Road. As I entered the centre, I was struck again by the fact that it looked exactly the same as I remembered it from my childhood. Everything, including the chandeliers, was unchanged. This was definitely a moment of déjà vu if ever there was one. One would have thought there would have been some changes in all that time, but no, and it remained as magnificent as ever. I went upstairs and sat by one of the doors where I used to sit with Grandmother Baa for prayer. It was a lovely evening, and the wind was blowing gently, so the muselin that covered each door were blowing just like years back; I felt a true sense of belonging.

Next we crossed the road back to that building where Grandmother had lived. We went upstairs and knocked on the door, hoping against hope that we could go in and look at her room once more. The couple that answered were quite shocked when we told them who we were and appeared reluctant to let us in at first. But in we went, and the memories flooded back. Eleven of us would congregate in that one bedsit, which had two bunk beds and an outside toilet. I was very fond of Grandmother; I could so clearly see her cooking for us in the corner of that room. Five adults—three uncles and two aunts—had lived in that one room. One could see what I mean about different worlds! But I should once again stress that these people—and myself, and my family in my early years—were happy and content. We had known no other way of life and appreciated the little things. For instance, there was a sweet shop downstairs owned by Baa's cousin. My aunt Begum would go down and buy a few cola bottles for my cousin, Shams, who used to visit over the summer holidays and me. Baa's cousin, Mohammad Ali Mama, would refuse to take the money, but she would insist that she would pay for the sweets. This would mean the world to us; the love was priceless. Shams and I shared some memorable times with grandma, Baa.

We returned to Amin's home that evening very aware of just how much things had changed in my time away from Uganda. Amir had moved to the UK in 1965, under different circumstances, thank goodness, and he had since returned several times. For me, not only was the volume of traffic on the roads so much greater, but also the condition of the roads was horrendous, with potholes everywhere. They looked more like those of Mumbai; they made for a rough ride and certainly contributed to my fatigue at the end of that day.

As we unwound, we prepared ourselves for another visit to the Ismaili Mosque, where, after prayers for this special occasion, food was going to be served. Then there would be dandia raas (Indian dancing). This was indeed such a special occasion, and it will remain embedded in my heart always, something that I will tell my children about for years to come. I would say I was very blessed.—Shukran" (thank God)—Amir, Amin, and all three sisters joined us, and we had a great time. Yet again, I looked thoughtfully across the road from the Ismaili centre, where Grandma Baa and family used to reside. These memories would never fade.

It made such an impression to see the people here living such peaceful, non-materialistic lives, while so many relatives had been lost in so many ways during the struggles that had ensued. I won't attempt a blow-by-blow account of every one of my 10 days back in Uganda. Rather, I will share with you some highlights in no particular order. I know a lawyer by the name of David Nmbale, a very charming young man and a truly genuine human being who studied law at Kent University and who also is known to my brother-in-law, Amin. David often stayed with us in Ascot while studying, and he is now very well established and works as a solicitor for the Ugandan Government. I had phoned him from the UK, telling him about the return visit we were about to make. We needed to hire a car, and we thought it better to make inquiries about this through someone we knew. When we returned to Amin's house after that first day, we were amazed to see, parked outside, a gleaming white 4 x 4 Toyota, complete with a driver, Michael. The surprise got even better. The whole thing—car, driver, and the time using it—was a gift from David, for the remainder of our stay. David knew how passionate I was about seeing my country again; I had told him of my love for this country and its people so often. However, his generosity was beyond belief.

First of all, we had to travel to Masindi Port, which was about 210 kilometers by road. At least this time the roads were tarmacked. Back in my childhood, they were in a horrible state, which did not exactly make things any easier for that final trip to the airport when we were fleeing our country. This time, as we sped back towards my home territory, every mile seemed like magic. As we drove along, I could see the farmers working in their corn and cotton fields. Young children fetched water from the wells on their bicycles with beaming smiles on their faces; some even waved to us with such innocence in their eyes. Buses were packed with people, and some passengers stood for miles but were content, not a complaint from them. They were more than happy to be able to get on the bus. Can you imagine that in the West? We are so spoilt that if a train or a bus is late by two minutes, our immediate reaction is to moan and groan. I knew we were really close when I recognised the crossroads just outside Masindi Port. There were just six more kilometers now, and then we were there, back in the village. My eyes filled with tears once more. I remembered so clearly how there had been just a dozen houses, consisting largely of corrugated iron sheets, when we left. Now, all these had become homes with shops (the shops at the front, with the living quarters behind). The whole area had turned into a very busy centre of commerce serving not just Masindi Port but also other villages within a five-mile radius; their residents would all come in for supplies such as paraffin, clothing, mosquito nets, and flour.

There was also a primary school with eight classrooms, again serving the children from all these villages. The external appearance of Masindi Port was not much different from the way I had left it, but the interiors of the properties, alas, had deteriorated very badly, which was very sad to see. Inside, large parts were derelict. They had not been properly maintained; the people left behind, who had taken them over, just didn't have the money, and it was all they could ever do to live from hand to mouth. I went into what had been my grandfather's shop and sub-post office for some 30 years, only to be struck by the sight of broken windows and severely limited goods in the shop. We had a friendly reception from the owners and we enjoyed speaking to some children who were there at the time. The children gathered around the car just as I used to when I was a child, because cars in that village were such a rare sight. I picked up a beautiful baby girl who was smiling at me, and her mother was more than glad to allow me to have a photograph taken with her.

But all the time I could not help thinking, all that hard work that my grandfather put into this shop and just look at the state of it now. But then I thought that I couldn't blame these people for that; for 40 years, they have barely existed, scarcely had enough money to survive. I felt deeply sorry for them, and the tears flooded through. We were there for about half an hour, and Amir was very supportive. To the rear of the property, we found the mango tree that I remembered from my childhood, except that it had now grown to around 60 feet. There was also a tree with the jambula fruit, which was a lovely fruit grown only in Africa. How fondly I treasured the memory of Grandad bringing in the mangoes when they had fallen from that tree, washing them and then handing them out to all the children.

Also outside the building was a patio area where I could remember Mum and Grandma doing the washing. On the other side of the patio there was cotton being dried on a mat. This cotton was eventually used to make quilts for the beds, for the few evenings during some parts of the year when it got slightly cold. My grandfather would make the cover first, fill it with cotton, and then sew the sides in order to make it into a quilt. We then walked slowly around this area, and then once we had left the shop, we strolled around the rest of Masindi Port, which stretched for about half a kilometre.

During this stroll, we had a remarkable meeting with a ninety-nine-year-old man who remembered my grandfather—and recognised me through my resemblance to Grandad. This man, Mwembe, was living behind the Jamatkhana that we used to visit for prayers. Faith was just as important then like it was today. Mwembe emerged out of the blue and began talking to us. Apparently, there was always considerable interest aroused in the little villages when a car with strangers came in, and we had been no exception. Mwembe spoke in Swahili and said, "Jumbo" (Hello). We shook hands, and he asked if I was related to the former postmaster. I could also speak a little Swahili, but a young man, who could speak it well, along with English, joined us and he translated. Together we managed to converse very effectively. Mwembe was anxious to emphasise to me that Grandad had been a very fair man, a true gentleman with a genuine concern for the welfare of all his customers, and everyone had loved him.

From here, we moved on to the pier that had been such a busy base for the fishing boats in my childhood, but which was clearly seeing considerably less activity now. I stood on the edge of Lake Kyoga, and the world stood still with me for a moment. I used to walk there with my grandfather and stand on the same spot, and many years later I was astonished to be doing this again. I stared at the breath-taking views across the lake and wondered about life and how much mine has changed now. I live in Ascot near Windsor, where I owned a boat on the river but hardly got time to use it, because life was so hectic, and here I was standing on lake Kyoga with all the time in the world. My eyes filled up with tears when, yet again, I had to walk away from it, leaving it all behind and not knowing when I would return.

We also visited the local cemetery, courtesy of another man, called Otty, whom we had met in the shop and who was my twin uncles' classmate. He came with us and showed us the graves of my grandfather and his brother, Shivji Ada, has also passed away in Masindi Port years ago. There were several other graves of people, but the only stone built one belonged to a young lad called Sultan. He was the son of Jamal Jetha.

As I prepared to leave Masindi Port, I looked at the houses, and a sense of sadness came over me. I could picture uncle Sherali standing in the front of the shop, waving good-bye when we were kids and when leaving for Masindi after the summer holiday. Every summer holiday, Sahera, Ferride, and myself would pack our bags to go over to Masindi Port and stay with him. The love and the joy the people had given me during this visit was something I would never forget. I was totally of two minds. I knew I had to leave because I had yet to get to Masindi, but at the same time my heart did not want to leave this beautiful little place. I felt such a sense of belonging. I waved good-bye to the local villagers and the wonderful children, and one little boy came running to me with a banana in his hand for me. I looked at his mother, and she told me that he had run all the way home to fetch me the banana. I was overwhelmed.

Michael then drove us to Masindi, where we arrived around 6.00 p.m. I had lived in Masindi Port for the first seven years of my life, and then the next two in Masindi, before we had to leave the country. As I entered Masindi, I recognised the road. This was the road by which we had left that night to flee Amin's Uganda. As we approached the town, my dad's building was the first one in town, so I had no trouble recognising Dad's former house, but by now it was mid-evening, so we did not consider it appropriate to make ourselves known to the present occupants at that time of day. I was dying to go inside, but had to hold myself back, because it would not have been fair to pester the residents at that time of the night. That property was no longer my dad's.

Instead, we asked Michael to drive us to the Masindi Hotel, the town's biggest, where we would be spending the next three nights. I was able to guide Michael in the right direction—I found that I still knew exactly where it was and how to reach it! The brain works wonders during childhood and absorbs incredible knowledge. I recalled how Dad would take me here as a child for the special ice cream treats. Ice cream was quite expensive in those days, and so a small tub would typically be bought for sharing. I would make sure I ate the ice cream slowly and enjoyed it. That was the height of ambition then, with the hotel itself looking so big and unreachable. Now, 40 years on, here I was, actually staying in Masindi's biggest hotel, and in its best room, and I could eat as much ice cream as I wanted to—but the desire was no longer there.

Our first visit the next day was to the hospital where my brother, sisters and I were all born. Now it was a centre for handicapped children, and once more I was all but overcome with emotion at what I found. It was always very sad merely to see a handicapped child, but in this case the experience was all the more painful for the very poor condition of the place. It had badly deteriorated through a severe shortage of funds. I found myself thinking, "Our children waste money, while in other parts of the world they have nothing, absolutely nothing."

As we left this building, I said to Amir, "I must go and see my father's house now, the house I lived in for two years." We found it easily enough, although it was now the base for an auto dealer, in addition to residential accommodation. Even before we had attempted to go in and make ourselves known, a man who turned out to be the landlord approached us in an aggressive manner. It seemed he suspected that I had come to repossess the house. This was not an entirely unreasonable suspicion; there were precedents because other Ugandan Asians had eventually returned to their homeland in the post-Amin era.

I stressed that this was not my purpose, and that I simply wanted to return to my former home for personal and sentimental reasons. The landlord took a lot of persuading. Next, he demanded some sort of proof that my story was genuine. I rose to the challenge and recalled a tiny window that was only visible from a certain part of the house, and about which no one but a longstanding occupant could have known. This convinced him, and his mood changed. He invited us in but still made it very clear that he really didn't want us there for more than five minutes or so.

Again I was struck by the severe deterioration in the condition of the building compared with how I remembered it from my childhood. It just didn't look the same anymore—it was all but devastated and looked as though a bomb had hit it. The toilets were broken, and everything was partitioned with cloth rather than proper walls. There were 15 people living in that house, I discovered, and we spoke briefly with them before leaving. I had very mixed emotions. As I looked around the veranda, which is an open-flooring area, I could see my younger sisters Shamira and Naffilla playing with their toys and dolls, when they were two and three. I could remember all the birthday parties we used to celebrate there. We also had a dining table where so many people had sat down for lunch. Anybody that came around, my father and mother would make sure that they sat down to eat with us.

Dad also used to invite the local counsellors to come and have lunch with us on many occasions. Unfortunately, it had been a short but very sweet visit back to a place that occupied such a special part of my heart. I did not want to overstay my welcome, and the landlord was already getting impatient.

In the clear distance to the back of the house, I could see a mango tree that I was very fond of climbing. My school friends and I would climb this tree for mangoes, and on one occasion I fell from the tree and injured my chin so badly that my mother has to rush me into hospital, and I needed stitches. In fact even today I have a scar underneath my chin, which reminds me of my fall. In all fairness I have no regrets; it was all great fun and part of growing up.

The return visit to my old school, Masindi Public School, was a very different affair. Structurally it looked exactly the same as I remembered it, albeit not in good condition, and even the main office inside had not changed. Remarkably, the man sitting at the table in this office looked up and said "Jamilla!" He was one of the school secretaries, Mr Isingoma Essau, who had no trouble in recognising me and recalling my name. He was overjoyed to see me and gave me a pat on my shoulder.

He remembered me, he said, because I had often been a naughty child! I would frequently arrive late for school. My mother would drop me at the top of the road and say, "Off you go." Once she was out of sight, I would do a U-turn and spend time wandering around the town. Mr Essau also asked after my late father, whom he knew as Rafiki, which had also been the name of his shop. He said the town missed him very much.

I asked him if I could see the headmaster, Mr Businge, who straightaway came out and shook my hand. He was a very fine young man and was very well spoken. He also called in a governor, Mr Kukenya Emmanuel, to join us. Mr Emmanuel made what amounted to a little speech. He said, "Thank you for coming to visit us. We are very glad to know that you were a student here and that you have made time to come back. We hope you can go back and tell people in the UK about the very poor condition of the school these days, and maybe inspire some help." I told him I would do my best to do so—and I am working with the school now.

Mr Businge dug out some very old school registers and showed me my name in them. I told him how my grandfather had been headmaster of this school from 1953 until he died, in 1955. Then he took us around the school so that we could be left in no doubt about its poor state. Once again, we found ourselves looking at a building characterised by broken windows and benches. The children had precious little stationery at their disposal—they wore torn clothing and no shoes. The school catered for children from seven to eleven and had some 250 pupils on its books. Some of them routinely walked a dozen miles to and from their homes each day. Amir and I were both very tearful when we learnt all this, and I found myself thinking, I have to do something to help these people, this school. I can and must do something to help.

My thoughts were interrupted by the sound of the school bell sounding for assembly. At this point, Mr Businge asked all the teachers to arrange for all the children to gather in the open yard area beneath the steps leading up to the school office. We stood at the top of these steps and listened as he told everyone that we were special visitors, and that "this lady went to school here".

This statement initially prompted some laughter amongst the children. They could not reconcile the sight of me—well dressed and seemingly prosperous—with their own lot as poorly dressed, poverty-stricken children attending a school that was seriously run-down and woefully short of resources. I assured them that I had indeed attended their school for two years, and with some difficulty, I declared, "I am really glad to be here, and I will try and help you as much as I can." In truth, I was so overcome with emotion that I could scarcely speak at all.

The twenty-minute assembly came to an end, and the children returned to their classes. Mr Businge continued his tour for us. He showed us the school playground, which had nothing, not even a netball ring, yet the children seemed so content. I was struggling to understand how that could be so. I visited my classroom and could clearly picture where I used to sit. Sitting next to me used to be a young boy, Anu, with whom I used to fight all the time. He never used to do his homework and always used to copy from me. The funny thing was that he was now living in London, and we were great friends with his family. We left the school determined to help them, and in the meantime we needed a bit of a break. Our experiences back in Uganda so far had been very moving and not a little poignant, and for want of a better term, we were beginning to feel emotionally drained.

We needed a little space, and we found the perfect solution with a visit to Murchison Falls. This may only be a "mini" Niagara, but it is still an awesome natural spectacle. It breaks the Victoria Nile, which flows across northern Uganda from Lake Victoria to Lake Kyoga and to the north end of Lake Albert, in the western branch of the East African Rift. At the top of Murchison Falls, the Nile forces its way through a gap in the rocks that is just seven metres (23 feet) wide. It tumbles 43 metres (141 feet) and then flows westward into Lake Albert. Some 300 cubic metres (11,000 cubic feet) per second of water cascades over the falls—squeezed into a gorge less than ten metres (30 feet) wide. It's the star attraction of the surrounding Murchison Falls National Park. We saw it all from top and bottom, first looking down on it all from above and then boarding a boat that took us to within a quarter of a mile of the falls at landing level.

On our last day in Masindi, we stopped outside what had been my father's shop, in the car. I looked at it for one last time and waved good-bye as we drove off. After Masindi, we moved to Kampala, where I had lived for about nine months as a child. Here we stayed for three nights in the Serena Hotel. What a magnificent hotel with wonderful staff and facilities. The whole place was like paradise, from restaurants to a wonderful fountain. One could sit by the fountain sipping coffee whilst listening to sound of water pouring out of the fountain. At that time there was someone incredibly special to my heart staying there, and I truly had some magical moments so very dear to my heart, which I have only shared with my family; Amir and I were truly blessed.

While we were staying at the Serena, we went out to a part of the city known as Kololo, the most prosperous part of Kampala. It had been a very upmarket residential area, established in the 1950s, and we enjoyed spectacular views from its high level. It included over a dozen embassies and ambassadors' residences.

Its significance for me was that it represented one more fondly remembered link with my childhood. When my uncles, Hassan and Hussein, had arrived in the UK 40 years ago, bound for the Honiton camp in Devon, they were collected by their cousin Ali, whose father Valimohamed used to own a wonderfully large house in Bukoto Street, Kololo. I had spent several days there as a child, and Ali Raza, one of my other cousins, used to teach us to swim. Moshin, another cousin, used to play cricket for the Ugandan National team. We returned to this property now—or rather, we parked outside its imposing gates. We explained who we were through the intercom button on the gate and asked if we could come in, just for a few moments. But the owners were adamant that they could not grant our request. It was private property—they didn't want us in, plain and simple. We went back to the Serena Hotel, where we met Amin, Adam, Naseem, Lucy, David and his wife, Geraldine, and their son, Lawrence. We had a pleasant meal at the buffet restaurant by the fountain and retired for the last night at the Serena.

After the Serena Hotel, we stayed for a day at Amin's house and visited the grave of Amir's grandfather, Jetha Bapa. Here there were people who recognised Amir because he looked so much like Bapa, my father in law. They inquired about his mother's whereabouts and dug out some photographs to show us. We recited the Suratal Fatiha (the first verse of the Holy Koran) by the graveyard. Amin and Amir cleaned up all the rubbish by the graves, and we drove around Kononi. This was where the majority of siblings on Amir's side had grown up and had gone to school. It was a nice little town with lots of memories.

And so my Uganda adventure drew to a close. All too quickly, it seemed, the time came for us to return to the airport and board a 4.00 a.m. Kenya Airways flight to Nairobi, where there was just a one-hour changeover period this time. Then we were back in the care of Virgin Flight, and the jumbo jet touched down at Heathrow at 6.00 p.m. local time.

That very same evening, we had scarcely returned home before we were off again for a big family reunion—and for the first showing of the one-and-a-half hour video that Amir had shot during our stay in Uganda. We went to Mum's home where we gathered in the lounge with all eyes on her large TV screen. Joining us for this very special occasion were our children; Ferride and his wife and four children; Shaida and her husband, and two of my children and one granddaughter. The following day we visited Bapa's house to show them the same video. Both the families were very excited to watch it.

As a travel agent, I have made many a trip to the Caribbean and all over Europe, but needless to say my visit to Uganda was in a class all of its own. It was very worthwhile. In so many ways, this was something completely different from any other journey I had ever made. I was so glad I'd done it. It was a mind-blowing trip, and I was on cloud nine for some time afterwards. But there was also an element of anxiety. I had the powerful, lingering thought that I simply had to do something for that school . . .

CHAPTER 16

A Tribute to My Parents and Uncles

I could not have asked for better parents. They worked so hard and made so many sacrifices for us. If I had the chance to live my life over again, I could never adequately repay them for all that they gave me.

Mum and Dad were strict, yes, but that was only because they really wanted us all to do well with our education and stand up on our own two feet. I concede that they did not spend as much time with us as we would have liked, because of their long working hours. They missed school plays and concerts, for instance, but they would always make time to collect our reports. Mum was out working at the Gloucester Road Hotel for three-quarters of the day, but she was always there for us when we came home from school. Without fail, supper would be ready for us, as would our school uniforms the next morning. Dad, on the other hand, was the provider, and so he had to work long hours. But both made sure that we never went without when it came to the really important things in life. Above all, the one thing we were never short of was love.

Dad was a self-taught man. More than anything, he taught himself so much about the world. When he left Uganda, he could speak fluent English. He read numerous books about various rulers, economic situations and all aspects of history. He read the Holy Quran, the Bible, and the Bhagavad Gita, and he taught us to accept all religions. There was, he told us, only one God, and the true religion was that of humanity—specifically, the ability to accept all people from different walks of life, and yet to be able to practise one's own faith. Throughout his life, he helped so many people but never wanted recognition. After his death in May 2006, countless people told us how he had helped them. This was a revelation to us—we had been totally unaware of this side of his life. He never spoke to anyone about his acts of kindness.

He was always anxious to ensure that we did the right thing. For instance, if we ever went out with him and we decided to park the car on the handicap bay—just for a few minutes because the parking slot was full—he would get mad. He would say that we were depriving someone else of his or her rights, and we should not be doing that. He got on well with everyone. He was known as Rafiki, which means "friend", because of his kindness to the locals. He understood their difficulties and helped them in whatever way he could. He would visit them in their homes and eat with them.

During my childhood, he was someone who commanded a great deal of respect because he was the eldest in the family. We siblings were close to him but would not joke with him. As time went on, we became friends to the point where we could talk to him about everything. He became very understanding and never resented having five girls and only one boy; he loved us all equally. I remember the time I was working in the bank, and there were tube strikes in the 1980s. He would wake up early and take me to my work place—some 40 miles. Work ethic was of paramount importance to him. He always made sure that we never took any unnecessary time off work.

We were always allowed to bring friends home. Dad loved Sundays because every fortnight he would have this day off. On such days, Mum would make breakfast, and we would all sit around the table and share it. That would be fine until something small would trigger a full-scale, but largely one-sided, debate. You can just imagine what it was like with six opinionated women around the table, and just the two male members, the poor things! There were lots of visitors on Sundays, too, mainly relatives. Mum would be a very busy lady in the kitchen. In Asian homes, food plays a very big part. The visitors would not be allowed to leave until they had eaten, and eaten well.

My father and Uncle Hadi had the shop for twelve years until one day they decided to sell it. After the sale, they bought a Post Office and shop in Mitcham Lane, Streatham. They ran the businesses for a number of years until they decided to sell them and go into semi-retirement. But Dad was so bored with retirement. He went to India with Mum on a holiday. During the years they took into their lives a lovely young lady of whom we are very fond, by the name of Banu. Banu and her lovely husband, Salim, had bought a flat in Mumbai to use as a holiday home and they generously left my parents the flat to stay in during this holiday. There son, Faizal, has been very helpful and spirited member of my family.

Dad had not been back to India since his sister's death, 20 years ago. At first Dad had grave reservations about returning, but we persuaded him otherwise, and off he and Mum went. They loved it. He had so much to say about it on his return. He was like a little child whenever he talked about his holiday; he became so excited as he recalled all their fond memories. Leopards don't change their spots, even when they are on holiday, and Mum told me how he had helped a lot of people there. He would stop during their travels and buy food for the people they saw sitting on the roadside. Both my parents were very open-minded and would allow us to bring our friends home, whether they were males or females. Amongst the males were our dearest friends Afghan, Bashir, Babu and Bowie. The girls included Effat. My parents got on so well with them all. I, too, can put my hands on my heart and say that these were our true friends, truly the best. My father trusted them to accompany us when we went out.

I have amazing memories of growing up, in particular around my early teens. I came across some old friends a few months ago, and we got to talking about schools. They all went to what the British call public schools, which are in fact the private schools, and we didn't. However, one of the girls said that although they may have gone to public schools, they always had the best time at the Karsans' home. She said Mr and Mrs Karsan—my parents—always conveyed so much love, and Mrs Karsan always had fresh food for everyone. In those days, I used to feel sad about not being able to go to a public school, but now I can sincerely say that although I recognise Dad's budgetary constraints, we have not done too badly! What we learnt at home from our parents was the best education anyone could have had. My teenage years were not without their difficult times, but we had a lot of love and happiness, which pulled us through. There was never any pressure to steer us into doing things for a career—so far as our parents were concerned, we could choose whichever field we wanted to go into—but working hard was an absolute must. My parents always taught us that everything worthwhile only came with hard work and honesty.

Dad and Mum played a major part in looking after the whole family. My twin uncles were only about a year old when my parents got married, and Mum nurtured them like a mother would. They in return gave a lot back, especially as we were all growing up together after the expulsion. Both Hassan and Hussein are chartered accountants and they have done a tremendous amount of voluntary work for the Ismaili Community. Hassan is married to a fine lady, Tazim, with two gorgeous girls, Nazia and Zaheeda. It is so strange because St George's Hospital has been so good to us over so many years, and Nazia is a Registrar doctor training to be a consultant neurologist at St George's. Zaheeda studied at Queen Mary and Westfield College, London, obtaining a degree in French and German and did very well, too, but is now ill, but has always been an inspiring and strong individual, never willing to surrender to her condition

Uncle Hadi's son, Rahim, who graduated from Oxford got married to a fine lady, Sharon recently. The wedding was held in San Francisco in a wonderful vineyard setting where all the extended families attended. We also attended another wedding, my cousins Hanif and Sheila's son's. Imran, whom we are very fond of, got married to a beautiful young lady, Alesha by the waterfront in Vancouver. Most of the relatives were present and it was a great bonding time for us all as many of us had not met up for years.

Since the expulsion the world has become a very small place and travelling long distances are not seen as challenges, which is a good thing. Hussein is married to Daulat, and they have two lovely girls, Shazia and Shabana. Shazia is in the final year for a master's degree in pharmacy and Shabana is starting a degree course in Economics at City University. Aunt Laila left home when she got married, and worked for a bank for many years. She married a businessman from Kampala, a gentleman from a very nice family quite well acquainted with my grandparents. Her husband, Uncle Nazmin, had been in England long before the expulsion of the Ugandan Asians. We often visited them in Baker Street, London, opposite Madame Tussauds—very exciting for us younger family members.

Shabnam Karsan, Zahra Govani,
Zaheeda Karsan and Alikhan Govani

Chapter 17

... And to My Grandparents

All of mine and Amir's grandparents came from India. They went to Uganda in their teens, around the 1910s, got married and established their lives in Uganda. They were taken to Uganda by the British, on a voyage that took several months by steamer. Typically, one male member of the family would leave the household in India and move to Africa, where he would work hard, become established, and then call for the rest of the family to join him. Then these families would open up their own shops, selling household goods, clothes, and food. My grandfather came with his two brothers, Shivji Ada and Abji Kaka, and they set up two shops next to each other. The whole family was very close; Uncle Abji's children and Uncle Shivji's only son, Babu, and Grandfather's family took great care of each other. Babu, as an only child, took great comfort and joy from being accepted into the larger family.

I grew up with my paternal grandparents, who lived with us and gave us great love and care. Grandfather Karsan, whom we called Kaka (a Gujarati word), was a quiet man and showed his love in very quiet ways. Grandmother Karsan, Baa, was a more lively personality and gave us great affection. My maternal grandfather, Ismail Tejani, passed away when I was only a baby, and grandmother Jena, whom we referred to as Nanima, was a very nice lady, although she was very strict. Unfortunately I did not get to know her very well in the early years of my life; this changed after we came to England. We would visit with my parents and spend a lot of time with her at her home in South

Harrow. She had a heart of gold and would fill bags up of goodies for Mum to take back with her. But I got to know her really well only after I got married—I would bring her back to stay with us. She was so good to us and would cook for me, but above all she had green fingers, and so she would take care of the gardening. She loved greenery and flowers; everything that she touched in the garden would flourish.

I remember a time when I invited Grandma Jena and Grandma Baa, and there was also another lady who was like a grandma to me, Rupa Masi. She, too, was from Masindi Port and was expelled by Amin. She came to live in Slough, which was near our home. I used to visit her regularly and loved her as much as if she were one of my own grandmothers. Once I invited all three of them around my house for the weekend, and they had a superb time, chatting non-stop. Then they wanted to pay a visit to the Brookwood Cemetery, where their loved ones were buried. As I took them there, I couldn't help but listen to their conversation. They asked each other if they thought they would end up at Brookwood themselves, and all of them seemed to agree that they would. However, this did not come about, because Grandma Jena died in Kenya and is buried in Kisumu, while Grandma Baa passed away in England and, yes, is buried at Brookwood. Grandma Rupa Masi died in Canada and is buried in Toronto.

The house where I live at the moment was bought in 1995. I brought along Grandma Jena to perform an opening ceremony, and she was the first person to enter this property once it was in our ownership. It has been a very lucky house for us, a peaceful home where I can relax after long hours of work. Grandma Jena must have had magical hands when she opened the door. As for Grandma Baa, what can I say? She played a big role in my upbringing. She loved all her grandchildren dearly, but I think—or at least I want to believe—that she loved me the most. She lived with us from our childhood, so there was always a really strong bond between us. She would feed everyone before she would eat herself. She loved life and people. Her sorrows were the death of my grandfather and Aunt Begum. These losses had a big effect on her life, but she somehow managed to live for her children and grandchildren.

She came with us from Uganda, but she arrived earlier than we did, so she was placed in another camp, in Devon. She was so high-spirited that she would not let anything get in the way. She stood by her sons and the family like the iron lady. She worked really hard in the shop, even during the cold winters despite the absence of any heating. The customers adored her. Occasionally she would catch a shoplifter, whom she would have thrown out by Dad or my uncle after retrieving the goods. She was a lady without fear. When I was a child, she would tell me stories about a man or woman on the moon, to put me to sleep, and it never failed! She would sometimes recite the Holy Ginans (hymns in an Indian language). She absolutely loved to do anything that would comfort us.

Grandma Baa was an excellent cook, but my favourite were the Indian sweets that she would make, called katla ladoos in Gujarati. My grandfather would get the ingredients, and both of them would make these katla ladoos in large quantities. Such was their generosity that these would be shared amongst all the people in Masindi Port. Who would swap this love of their grandparents for anything else? The joy of sitting on their laps and being fed these ladoos was sheer magic. If only I could go back in time and live that part of my life again—those were incredibly happy years.

They were fun years, too. Grandma Baa would sit by the window in the evenings and wait for her sons to come back. I would laugh at her and say, "My father is old enough and can look after himself, so you do not need to worry about him; he will find his way home okay." She would simply reply, "You will never understand this until you have your own children."

I have subsequently learnt a million times over that her comment is so, so true. I have precisely the same habit. Actually, I don't just sit by the window if the children are late home from somewhere; I upgrade to panic mode and start pacing the floor, wearing the carpet out, wondering where on earth they are and why they are so late. And when they laugh at me, I tell them that they will be just the same one day! As Grandma Baa got older, she became weaker but carried on cleaning and cooking; she just would not give up. Until one day she fell and broke her hip. She was rushed into hospital, and this was when we realised that this woman, who had been our strength throughout life and who had carried so many burdens on her shoulders with a smile, had become physically tired and weak. Those strong hands that used to feed me were now shaking with soft, loose skin. Emotionally, it was very difficult to adjust to this new situation; we found it so hard to accept that our beloved Grandma, who had been such a pillar in our lives, could be anything other than strong.

We visited her in hospital nearly every day but each time we would get up to go home, she wanted to come with us. We would convince her that she was only there for a few days. One Sunday, whilst she was still in hospital, the whole family had taken part in a sponsored walk, in Hyde Park in London, organised by the community to raise funds for designated charities. On the way back from the walk, we decided to stop at St George's Hospital in Tooting, to see Grandmother. I took her a few bounty chocolates, which she loved; they were her favourite. When we arrived, she looked very well and enjoyed the chocolate. We had a good laugh with her. As we were leaving, Amir and the children made their way downstairs to the car, but she got one of the nurses to call me. I went back into her room, and she smiled at me, so I asked her if she wanted anything, to which she replied, "No, I don't want anything; I just wanted to see you again." Not in a million years did I think that it was the last time I would see her. I kissed her on her cheek and told her that I would be back in a couple of days. As I walked out of the hospital I distinctly remember being very happy because she looked so well, and I thought she would be home in no time.

This was not to be, because God had different plans for her. We dropped by Mum and Dad's, who were also under the impression that Baa looked really well, because they had visited her that morning. My twins were only two years old, so Amir and I decided that we had a very tiring day at Hyde Park and should go home, retiring for the night. At around four o'clock in the morning, I got a phone call from Dad giving me the sad news that Baa had passed away peacefully. I burst out crying. She was the pillar of our family and I could not think about life without her. The whole family was devastated. She is buried at Brookwood cemetery, which I regularly visit. I often sit by her grave and talk to her. People might think I am mad, but I am sure she can hear me. She might not be with us in person, but she definitely is in spirit, and in all the things she taught us throughout life.

Chapter 18

Canada Calling

Canada also figured prominently in the aftermath of Amin's expulsion order. At this time, the Canadian embassy in Uganda was only interested in people who were educated or those who were working and providing for the families. In many cases, there was at least one family member who met the Canadian entry criteria, which facilitated emigration of other family members.

Amongst the "early birds" was my cousin, Nazmin Nanji. His parents, Sadru bhai Nanji, Aunty Gulshan, and sister, Shenaz, were left behind. Nazmin was on the first Air Canada flight to Edmonton. He settled in Edmonton, Canada, and then acted as sponsor for his parents and his sister. Sadru and Gulshan now live in Toronto and Shenaz continues to live in Edmonton. Back in Uganda, they were settled in Fort Portal. We used to spend lots of summer holidays there. Gulshan aunty was a fantastic dressmaker who used to spoil us all with her dress making skills and we always came home with new dresses.

Some of our extended family are also settled in Canadian, in cities such as Vancouver, Calgary and Edmonton. Those who moved there included Fidai bhai, Aunty Roshan Hanif, Shams, and Rahim. At first they lived in England in Rawtenstall, a lovely little town in Lancashire, Rahim was only a baby then, eventually Hanif decided that he wanted to move to Edmonton, which was made possible through Uncle Sherali's sponsorship. This is the same uncle who was evacuated with my father and Uncle Hadi to Austria. Dad and Uncle Hadi eventually joined us in England, but Uncle Sherali and my Aunt Rashida settled in Edmonton. He has three boys, Farhad, Sameer and Hussein, and a lovely daughter, Farhana, all born in Canada. We have very much bonded with our cousins and our siblings adore them. To think we are miles apart, totally brought up in different parts of the world yet to have such love amongst all is an incredible thing. Hence I always say 'shukran', God has been very graceful.

Hanif got to married Sheila, and they have two children, Imran and Natasha. My cousin Nazmin married Nargis, another Asian expelled from Uganda, and they have three children, Karim, Salimah and Salman. All these kids have now grown up. Nazmin's sister, Shenaz, married a really nice man called Kim and has settled in Edmonton and have two children, Safeer and Rizzy. Hanif's brother, Rahim, also got married and is settled in Edmonton.

One of the brothers of my grandfather, Abji Kaka, and his family moved to Canada, too. They had been living in Fort Portal in Uganda. They bottled a fizzy drink known as Portello. Noorali Ada, Fatu bhabhie, their son Azim, and two daughters, Shenaz and Yasmin, settled in Vancouver. Azim is married to Shamira, a fine young lady, and has a son, Adam. Shivji Ada's son, Babu, emigrated to Canada and is living in Edmonton with his wife.

Uncle Sadru and Aunty Roshan, with their son, Imitiaz, and daughter, Rozy, settled in Calgary. Uncle Sultan and Aunty Farrida, their son, Bobby, and daughter, Salima remained in Vancouver, as did Uncle Mansoor and Aunty Sakar, Aunty Doli, Ashraf uncle and family. Aunty Suli, Aunty Parin, and their families all settled in Canada, too. Unfortunately, we lost Uncle Sultan after a battle with cancer; this was such a tragedy because he was a very nice, young, good-looking man who was full of life. We also lost Uncle Mansoor, of whom I had been very fond as a child. I used to go to Fort Portal during the school holidays and Uncle Mansoor and Abji kaka and kaki would really spoil me.

Aunty Nabat and Amir bhai and their two children, Alikhan and Femida, first came to England and lived with us in Rowfant Road, Balham, for about three months. Then they were sponsored to move to Canada by one of their relatives, and they are now settled in Edmonton. Alikhan's children, Zulificar and Lailla, also Femida's daughter, Fariya have grown up, but we have made sure that all the cousins keep in touch so that if we are no longer here, they know their cousins and can maintain the bond between themselves.

As the world has become smaller with the major expansion and improvement of air transport, so it has become so much easier for today's children to travel widely. This is such a huge bonus for them—everything is just a flight away, and so families can visit each other much more frequently than used to be the case a generation or two ago. In stark contrast, my grandfather Kaka came to Africa when he was in his teens, and although he always wanted to revisit his home in India, the remainder of his life went by without him ever actually achieving this. For one thing, everything still seemed so far away in those days, and for another, in those days, the business of raising money for a flight was akin to securing a loan for a house.

My dad's brother, Akbar, was studying in Nairobi at the time of the expulsion. He finished his studies, got married to a young lady called Naseem, and joined us in England. He lived with us for a year or so before he, too, emigrated to Edmonton. He studied to become a land surveyor, as there were more job opportunities in that field in Canada, and so it made more sense for him and Aunty Naseem to grasp that opportunity and commit their future to that country.

After a few years Akbar and Naseem moved to Vancouver, where they had a son called Sajid. Then tragedy struck. In 2006, the couple were flying to Dubai and stopped in London to visit us. During that visit, Naseem complained about a pain in her shoulder. When they returned to Vancouver, Naseem was examined, and to everyone's horror she was diagnosed with cancer—and it had been discovered too late. We all were devastated. Such a beautiful young life—she was only 54 years old. A few months later, she passed away after losing her final battle. My sister, Shaida, was already in Canada; she had gone over a few days earlier to visit her in hospital and help Uncle Akbar out with the hospital visiting. Prior to that, Mum had also been there to help out around the house and with the hospital visiting.

I joined my father and Sahera on the flight across the Atlantic to attend the funeral. Strangely, on our way there, Sahera and I were both concerned to notice that Dad appeared to be a little aloof. We assumed that it was the shock of my aunt's death. He was very cold on the flight and hardly ate a thing. Then the following day, we all attended the funeral, and Dad continued to be very quiet.

It was a very crowded affair. There were hundreds of people, partly because there were two funerals taking place concurrently, and also because a lot of our family members from Calgary and Edmonton—along with all our other relatives in Vancouver—had made the trip. It was an extremely sad occasion. After all the ceremonies finally came to an end, Dad was so tired that he decided to retire for the night. Whenever he visited Vancouver, he always stayed at Hanif's house because he felt comfortable there, and so that is where he was staying now.

Early the following morning, he came over to Uncle Akbar's house for breakfast, and then he left for England. He made the return flight on his own—something which we would never have allowed had we only known then what was in store.

Chapter 19

Lincolns

I had grown up in a family that put an enormous amount of emphasis on education. Both Amir and I felt that we should apply this to our children, especially considering the way this world was moving in the areas of employment and the hardships future generations were going to endure in these areas of work and stability.

Farzana wanted to study law from a very young age. She enjoyed school, where she became head girl of the Brigidine School in Windsor whilst studying for her A levels. She was a music scholar and practiced singing and playing the piano, which was a natural talent, but she needed a stable career that would carry through the future.

After passing her A levels in music, history, and German, she decided to study law at Brunel University, which she accomplished in a few years. Then she studied for a couple of years more, to become a barrister. She worked extremely hard and achieved her goals, and for us, as parents, it was a dream come true with the grace of God. I was pleased she was very humbled by this degree she had achieved.

During her graduation at Brunel University, I was doing poorly with colon cancer, but I made sure that Amir, myself, the twins and mum were there to see her get her degree. Her grandparents on her dad's side would have been there but weren't well enough to travel. We missed them and my dad at this incredible occasion. However, it was a long day, and I could barely sit, so we attended only part of the graduation ceremony.

A year later, I was in high spirits with my health a lot better, so both Amir and I were invited to Lincoln's Law Chambers, where we spent the day in London near the High Court, and it was amazing. Farzana met us near the High Court of Justices and took us to her office at St Paul's, where she had landed in her first job with a company called Melton's Legal. Here we met up with her wonderful boss, Oxford educated Mr. Vassos, who was an amazingly down to earth and was a very well-spoken gentleman. He was friendly with a very likeable personality. He welcomed us straight away and sang Farzana's praises. The office was beautiful, overlooking St Paul's cathedral.

I truly thanked God that Farzana had found such a boss who helped her into her job so quickly, and she could learn so much from him. My little baby was now working in central London, and when she first got this job, I was so worried about how she would cope living away from home and working in London. However, I could see that she was doing a fine job and had gained a lot of confidence.

She then took us to buy the gown and the wig she had ordered for the ceremony at Lincoln's Inn. As we walked inside the shop, the gentleman brought out the wig, which she put on to see if it fit her head. This was truly a magical moment, and it was the first time I could see tears rolling down Amir's face. He looked at me, and I could hear him say, "Thank God she has made it. All those years of truly hard work will finally see a good end."

We were then taken to the law chambers, where we all had to queue in an orderly manner. Farzana was called in to sign in the official register, which meant that she was officially a barrister. There were very many important people like Charles the First, and many others who had already signed the register, were members of Lincoln's Inn. We then had pictures taken followed by the graduation. The joy on parents' faces as their child was getting their certificate was very emotional. Some had saved money for many years to send their children to England to achieve this. I spoke to a couple of parents who sat opposite us for the evening dinner, and they told us that they had been saving for months to buy their air ticket to come to the graduation service.

During the day, there was a church service at Lincoln's Chapel, which we attended. It was very moving because the vicar stood up and said to the students that the profession they had chosen was one that protected human beings, and one should always choose the righteous path and not be misled by earning wealth with evil ways. Farzana's music came in handy because she recited a hymn, which she was taught at school and the vicar was impressed with her voice. We met up with many lawyers and barristers who had made it in this world.

The festivities came to an end after the evening supper. Oh, what a remarkable day! On our way home, Amir and I could not stop talking about this event. This was a time when one realized that if one planted humility, one would reap greatness. Most of all, if one planted hard work, one would reap success—but only with God's grace.

Farzana's graduation at Brunel university.

Chapter 20

Another Family's Story

The stories of terror that preceded the great Amin-inspired escape out of Uganda, and the heroic fashion in which lives were rebuilt from scratch in foreign lands are amazing. During my research for this book, I have had the privilege of sitting down with members of the Lakhani family and hearing their story. I think you will agree that theirs is a truly moving account—one which demonstrates once again that "out of darkness cometh light", and one which has been replicated so many times over the past 40 years in so many ways.

Our friends Naseer and Zuleikha's family went through a similar situation to ours. Naseer's parents, Sadrudin Hassam Lakhani and Gulshan Lakhani, were in Kampala when news of the expulsion order broke. Luckily, Naseer, Badru and Shelina, their siblings, were already in England, having come over for their education. They had worked hard and built the foundations for a future for their families for generations to come.

In 1952, the Lakhani brothers established a bakery in Kawempe, near Kampala that was very successful—the just reward for the endless hours of sheer, hard work they put into the enterprise. As times got better, they conceived other ideas, and in 1956, Sadru Lakhani and his brothers invested in a biscuit factory called Mukisa Biscuits. The family continued to do extremely well and deservedly built on their earlier success. Despite their increased wealth, Sadru Lakhani and Gulshan Lakhani remained very humble and helped many people in various ways.

Sadru and Gulshan became a leader of our community—the Ismaili community—and served everyone to the best of their abilities. When the expulsion came, the army got out of control. With law and order consigned to history, soldiers broke into the factory and demanded a large amount of money. They raided the warehouses and wrenched open boxes in a desperate bid to find cash. This experience terrified the family, with no one feeling remotely safe in these transformed circumstances. Sadru, Gulshan, and other members of the Lakhani family moved into the Grand Hotel, which they regarded as a sort of a safe haven. They felt it highly dangerous to return home in case the army came there in further raids. They asked their housekeeper to pack a couple of suitcases and take them to the hotel. The housekeeper disapproved of Amin's regime and was glad to do whatever she could to help the Lakhanis. She, too, was very upset, as someone who had been very happy working for the family for so many years and having seen the children grow up.

Sadru was considered to be in particular danger, given his wealth and his status as the head of a community that was being expelled. His family was also regarded as being at great risk, by association. However, being a very good humanitarian, he did not want to flee until every member of his community had safely left the country first.

Nonetheless, a warrant was out for his arrest, and his family and friends insisted that he should flee just as soon as he could. He was in no doubt that he would not be spared if caught, and that Gulshan was in danger, too. After much debating, he agreed to go and purchased the air tickets for the UK. Both Sadru and Aunty left the hotel in a bus and bid emotional good-byes to everything they had worked so hard for—the house, the factory, the cars, and more. On the way to the airport, they could see that the two buses that were ahead of them were being searched at gunpoint. Men with machine guns, wearing the Ugandan army uniform, were asking everyone if there was someone called Sadrudin Lakhani on the bus. They did not find him on the first two, but as the soldiers approached the third, Sadru ducked beneath his seat. His fellow passengers knew who he was, but they all denied any knowledge of him being on the bus. It worked—but the consequences if Sadru had been discovered after that deceit do not bear thinking about.

They got to Entebbe and kept as low a profile as they could around the airport, because they were acutely aware that the army were still looking for Sadru Lakhani. Sadru and Gulshan boarded the plane, and as it took off they breathed a big sigh of relief, counting their blessings in the belief that they were now safe. Alas, they were still a long way from safety. The couple was flying on East African Airways, and the flight was to stop in Nairobi. The army had realised that Sadru Lakhani was on this flight. Through a telex sent by Amin's men, Jomo Kenyatta Airport was alerted to stop Sadru and Gulshan once their plane had landed there. At the same time, however, some friends of the couple had alerted others in influential quarters in Nairobi about their imminent arrival at the airport, and they had requested help in delivering them to safety by enabling them to board any flight destined for Europe. Kenya, being an East African country, could not provide immunity for the couple, and if they were caught they would have to return to Uganda. But escape to any European country would mean safety at last.

In Nairobi there was someone waiting to guide them to safety, and as soon as they had rendezvoused, the couple were escorted out to a transit lounge, where they could wait until they caught another flight. The tickets to the UK were also waiting for them, but this time they were with Swissair. This flight was not going out until the evening, so they had to be patient and go into hiding for a few hours. Throughout this stage of their ordeal, a well-known member of the Ismaili community, the late Sir Eboo Pirbhai, helped them. After a wait that must have seemed liked a lifetime, the friend took them to Nairobi Airport, quickly checked them in and got them boarded onto the Swissair flight. The flight was stopping in Zurich for many hours, but this did not matter. Eventually the flight took off for the UK, and that was when they could pinch themselves and count their blessings for being alive and escaping torture from Amin's army. After another long and tiring flight, Sadru and Gulshan arrived at London's Heathrow Airport. As we had been, they were still dressed in their summer clothing, but the weather in England was cold. They were lucky because they had their family members—Naseer, Badru, and Shelina—already in England, and so they were able to join them.

So it was mission accomplished. They had escaped from Uganda and reached safety—but that country and the horrific events that had engulfed it remained at the forefront of their minds. It could hardly have been any other way after such a life-changing experience, but their awareness was heightened by daily coverage in the English newspapers about the torture being inflicted on the people they had left behind—and how things were becoming even worse. Sadru was a businessman who eventually came to terms with the loss of his possessions, and he reinvested in other projects in the UK. They joined up with extended family members to work together and opened up a shop in Wandsworth called Rockcastle, importing denim from Hong Kong with the help of Gulshan's father, Pir bhai Ladha, who was a very astute man. They subsequently supplied stores on Carnaby Street and the King's Road, which through their own hard work and with God's blessings earned them further prosperity. Away from business, Sadru and Gulshan also continued to help people in various other ways.

In the 1980's, Sadru's family acquired two hotels but unfortunately fell. They were the victims of the recession of the 1990s. The family worked like Trojans to achieve such results, and nothing came easy. Sadru then returned to Kampala, Uganda, to repossess the business, however ill health set in, and sadly Sadru eventually lost his life after a long battle with Parkinsons-PSP. His family now lives in a beautiful property in Putney. Sadru was truly someone to look up to and a lot of people admire him for how he dealt with the expulsion in getting so many people out of Uganda at the risk of his own life.

Naseer got married to Zuleikha, a young lady whom I met at St George's and am great friends with now. Zuleikha came from Mwanza, the capital of Sukumaland in Tanzania. Her father, Talib, was a Freemason who had moved to England in 1971 from Mwanza, for Zuleikha's education. Ebrahim Talib wanted to send her to the Royal Masonic School. He had organised a loan to buy a Bata Shoe agency, a franchise that he already owned a branch of in Mwanza. Previously Ibrahim was the inspector of the Agakhan School's East Africa branch, having graduated from Poona and Cambridge University. However, prior to starting the business he suffered a massive heart attack, which ultimately proved fatal. This left Zuleikha and her mother, who were both distraught. Zuleikha's mum, Zehra bai, a truly lovely human being and a lady, worked all hours to fulfil her husband's ambition of educating Zuleikha, their only child.

Life can work in such strange ways. I met this lovely family through Zuleikha's gorgeous daughters, Alysia and Anoushka, who went to school with my twins at St George's in Windsor Castle. We have built up such a friendship over the years that we are now inseparable, in good times and bad. Zuleikha's mum, Zehra bai, was also very close to us. My children adored her like their own grandmother, and she gave them that unconditional love that only a grandma can provide. Farzana developed an amazing bond with her, confiding and sharing so much. If Zehra bai had not seen her for a few days, she would ask me where she was. She was a wonderful, kind, generous human being who brought up Zuleikha whilst sacrificing so much on her own account in the process. There were times when she was holding down no fewer than three different jobs in order to make ends meet. Her employment included twelve years at Debenhams, the famous department store. A few years ago, she had a fall that led to her becoming significantly less mobile, but she retained her charm and humour for all that. Naseer and Zuleikha took great pride in looking after her. Zehra now lived for her lovely two granddaughters, Alysia and Anouhska, whom she encouraged to do well with their education. When they both reached university, she missed them terribly. Her life's journey was reaching its end; she had accomplished everything she wanted to accomplish and she kept saying she wanted to rejoin her husband.

One night last October, Zuleikha phoned to tell me that Zehra bai had been rushed into hospital, and her heart was failing. She remained in the hospital for a few days but had clearly lost the will to fight. She died very peacefully, and until her last breath she kept on praying to herself. If only there were more people in this world like her. She was an absolute gem who has imparted so much knowledge and wisdom to those she left behind. Life was so full of struggles and hardships for her, but she never contemplated anything resembling defeat. Always she lived with faith in God, humanity, and dignity—priceless qualities that she has passed on in abundance to her granddaughters, Alysia and Anoushka, and I must say to all my children.

Another eyewitness account of the incredible period that followed Idi Amin's expulsion announcement, and its amazing aftermath, has been supplied to me by David Nambale, my dear, charming Ugandan brother who was just six years old when the Asians were thrown out of Uganda. David is a Ugandan who has studied Law at Kent University and is now working for the Ugandan government in Kampala. He has a beautiful wife, Geraldine, and two gorgeous children, Lawrence and Mathew.

One evening over supper during a recent visit to England, David recalled the chilling sequence of events his family had suffered during Amin's presidency. Amin spared no one, and even after the Asians had left the country, the black Ugandans were targeted, through no fault of their own, and tortured. David shared his father's experience when at one time he worked as a diplomat for the Ugandan High Commission in New Delhi, India,

David recalled the "total anarchy" that broke out in the entire nation after the expulsion of Asians. No semblance of conventional law and order remained, and Amin's army were highly corrupt and greedy. Nothing stopped them from snatching other people's possessions. David said the atmosphere was one of absolute terror, fear and intimidation. He remembers how, at the age of six, he was told to keep away from men in uniform. It was explained to him that instead of exercising their duty to protect the people of Uganda, their greed for power was achieving precisely the opposite. At one point, his uncle, a police officer, knocked on their door to pay them a visit. David's mother opened the door to let him in, but David, remembering what he had been told about men in uniform, and not realising that this officer was family, ran for his life in sheer terror. His mum ordered him to come out from under his bed where he was hiding and greet his uncle, but she first had a lot of explaining to do in convincing David that his uncle was not the same as the others.

Each day was a potential battle for survival. David's father was protected to a certain extent because he was working for the government, but even he did not feel secure and safe. One day his father failed to return home after work. His mother and family were extremely worried, and there was no way of contacting him because there were no mobile phones in those days. Hours passed and there was still no sign of him. By this time the family were in a panic, but all they could do was wait. The next day someone from Mulago Hospital visited their home and informed David's mum that her husband was lying in hospital with severe injuries. She rushed off to the hospital and had her worst fears confirmed, discovering that he had sustained severe injuries at the hands of the soldiers. It transpired that on his return from work, he was driving a private Peugeot car, to which the army had taken a fancy. They stopped him and demanded the keys, but David's father resisted, so they brutally pulled him out of the car at gunpoint and kicked and beat him. They took the car and left him to die, lying on the roadside. Luckily, a passing motorist spotted him and took him to the nearest hospital. David's father was lucky to survive, and when the dust had settled, they were left with the thought that if such a thing could happen to a diplomat, what chance would the poor locals have? David also told me how the economy had reached a state of total collapse. The factories ceased production, and with the price of food and other daily needs soaring, shops were looted. There was widespread poverty, along with a growing number of torture incidents. Neighbouring countries stopped trading with Uganda. So many Ugandan people lost their lives.

As well as David's testimony, I personally remember another incident in Masindi that involved a family who was very well known to us, and whose son loved motorbikes. Avery was a handsome 21-year old man, who was full of life. One day, a group of soldiers in a lorry began following him. He tried to get away, but they chased him and succeeded in stopping him. They wanted his motorbike, but Avery resisted. The soldiers let him get on the bike and ride off, only to resume the chase. This time there was a gruesome outcome, with the soldiers engineering a crash whereby their lorry collided with Avery on his motorbike and crushed him to death. Such cruelty was unbelievable—and yet was happening constantly in Amin's Uganda.

Alysia, Zahra, Anoushka

Chapter 21

My Dear Sister's Tragic Battle

Life is full of ups and downs, it is said, and in my family's case I think I can safely go along with that sentiment! I suspect that few if any lives are completed without experiencing an immense range of emotions, from the deepest sorrow to the greatest happiness. My biographer's father used to say, "Life is a desert of strife with oases of peace." How true. The day is never too far away when we are confronted with a new problem or are tested by a new challenge, and we all have our different ways of dealing with these situations. Some of us instinctively hide through fear rather than face up to problems, while others try to keep a brave face and tackle them head-on. There is no right or wrong answer to such things, but time, in one way or another, is not only a great healer but also a means of making us stronger and teaching us all to cope that much better with everything that life has in store for us.

In my family's case, we have certainly had our fair share of happiness, but we also have our tragedies. At first we found these very difficult to understand, but as time has passed, we have learnt to recognise, accept, react, and adjust. One very sad and difficult element of our lives has been the very serious, long-term illness suffered by my dear sister, Naffilla, who has been a victim of anorexia for so many years now. Anorexia nervosa, to give it its full title, is an eating disorder characterised by an obsessive fear of gaining weight. (Anorexia is simply a medical term for lack of appetite.) Anorexia nervosa has many complicated implications and is generally regarded as a long-lasting illness that can never be truly cured. The big hope is that it can be managed over time, and that is our hope with Naffilla.

Naffilla is the most beautiful human being I have ever known. Not only is she beautiful in appearance but she is also such a kind and gentle soul. For many years, she had long dark hair, which enhanced the beauty of her large brown eyes and charming personality. Anywhere she went, she would make heads turn. She loved wearing yellow, which really suited her. She was very fond of the singer Simon Le Bon, and when she was still only fifteen years old, she was approached by one of his band members as she sat in the front row of a theatre. He asked her if she would be interested in modelling for their new video, which was for their next new song. Being very shy, she declined the opportunity.

Two years earlier, when she was thirteen, we first noticed that she was cutting down drastically on her food, but at that stage we just thought it was part of the business of growing up. We had never heard of anorexia then, so at the outset we were blissfully unaware of such an eating disorder and that people had died from it. We gradually discovered that, through the obsessive fear of gaining weight, its sufferers lost their appetite completely—together, tragically, with a distorted self-image and a great reduction in self-confidence. In Nafilla's case, it has indeed developed to the point where it clearly threatens to be lifelong, with no cure. Our best hope is merely that the condition can be managed over time. It began with her refusing to eat food, leading to a conspicuous loss of weight. She developed an obsession about calorie counting and fat content in the foods that she ate. She would even avoid eating with the rest of the family. By the time we as a family realised that this was more than simple dieting, she had already lost several stone and had to be admitted into hospital for treatment. She initially refused to go in and we had to force her.

First she was fed regularly to restore her to a healthy weight, and this was a really heartbreaking experience for us. She was suffering physically, and we were all suffering mentally. It truly had a devastating effect on us. She remained in Atkinson Morley Hospital for three months. After her weight was restored—a process that took the full three months of her stay—she then needed to be treated psychologically. She had therapy to eliminate or reduce behaviour and the thoughts that had originally led to the fundamental eating disorder. Naffilla still didn't recover fully, but she was allowed to come home because she had coped well with the treatment. As time went on, she learnt to live with this awful affliction. The doctors advised us that she would be better able to cope with it if she were living on her own, so she moved into her own flat, where she learnt to live her life her way. Mum would pick her up every day in the afternoon, and Dad would drop her back home in the evenings. She was such a good girl in the sense that she would help Mum cook and clean. Also, whilst my nephew, Waseem Salman, and my nieces, Shabnam and Yasmin, were growing up at Mum's, Naffilla would always be there to give a hand with the children. Indeed, she played a little mother to them. She had a heart of gold and was also helping the elderly in the neighbourhood with their shopping.

However, as time went on, the eating disorder took its toll once more, and she began to lose weight again. In the meantime, I had gotten married and consequently was not so directly involved. Shaida, Ferride, Mum, and Dad dealt with it. My two other sisters, Sahera and Shamira, were on hand, too. It reached the point where Naffilla had to return to hospital, having lost so much weight again. We began to fear the very worst—that we might lose her. If this illness is not treated, it can lead to very serious complications such as heart conditions and kidney failure, which in turn can lead to death. This time Naffilla was admitted to Atkinson Morley's Hospital in Tooting, South. Shaida, Mum, and Dad would visit her every day, and the rest of us twice a week. We were heartbroken because we genuinely believed that her organs were going to fail.

But with the grace of God, she survived this horrible period in her life. The poor girl suffered so much once again from being force-fed. In particular, she developed swollen ankles and had violent mood swings. It was a big mental strain for the whole family, and by now we all had other family commitments. Through thick and thin, however, Shaida and Ferride, with my two sisters, were always there for her and to support Mum and Dad. Nizam, Shaida's husband, was very understanding about how much time she was spending with Naffilla every day; Shaida was like a second mum to her. Doctor Crisp at Atkinson Morley advised us all to have family therapy. This involved the whole family seeing the same therapist at the same time as the patient, so that we could exchange views about the illness. It also made the family more aware of the issues around Naffilla and anorexia. Of all the difficult chapters in our lives, this was one of the hardest. It was so painful for us when we saw just how much Naffilla was suffering. We would usually come out of therapy in a very emotional state and feeling utterly drained. At times we would even feel full of guilt as we traced our lives back to when it all started for Naffilla. We would torture ourselves with the question: Was there anything we could have done to save her from going down this path?

Then we lost Dad through cancer and we were all devastated, but Naffilla and Shaida unselfishly supported Mum throughout this pain. Through all this, I believe Shaida somehow managed to grieve, but Naffilla did not have time to grieve over Dad. Shaida had wonderful support from her husband, Nizam, and her children, Imran and Nabilla. Nizam had already lost his lovely father through cancer, so he understood the pain. One minute Dad was there for Naffilla, giving so much support, dropping in at her home and so on, and then all of a sudden, in the space of just three or four weeks, we had lost him. We all missed him terribly, but for Naffilla with her anorexia, the world turned upside down. She carried on as best she could for a few years, keeping herself busy with Mum until Naffilla's own private hell began yet again.

In 2011 her weight had shrunk to four and a half stone, and she found herself once more being admitted into hospital. This time she spent six months at St George's, also in Tooting, being tube-fed throughout that period. Once again Shaida and Mum visited her every day, and the rest of us visited her twice a week. Her weight was so low that her thinking became irrational. She kept crying, and although we did our best to support her, we felt that we, too, were sinking with the pain of seeing her suffer. The staff was absolutely brilliant. Naffilla is a very kind soul who gets on well with everyone, and they loved her.

By now, all our children were that much more grown up, and they were close to Naffilla and were able to help her that much more. Naffilla would never forget their birthdays and things like their exam dates; she was always there for them, protecting them like a hawk. Through being in hospital, she became very close to my daughter Farzana in particular. Farzana made sure she visited her sick aunt at least three times every week. Nabilla truly understood Nafilla and would take her little one, Hana to visit her. Hana would sit on the bed and cuddle Naffilla. But this time the process took longer for Naffilla to get better. It became apparent that she wanted to give up, and we were really frightened for her now. She was our baby sister—how could we possibly allow her to give up? Mum, Shaida, Ferride and Farzana would spend endless hours with her at the hospital. We all did everything in our power to stand by her and support her. Besides Mum herself, Shaida in particular played a very motherly role to her. This turn for the worse was the last thing we wanted to witness.

As time went on, it got harder still. Shaida and Naffilla would meet up with consultants and the anorexia team, whom I cannot praise highly enough. They were brilliant throughout, with all their hard work and dedication to my dear sister's well being. In fact, I must say that St George's Hospital has got to be one of the very best. I cannot fault their endless hard work. We saw this when my grandma was there; we saw it again when my dad was there, and whilst my mum was there; and now we were witnessing it again with Naffilla. Eventually, after many months, Naffilla was discharged from St George's and transferred to Atkinson Morley. There were more hard months to follow, with family therapy teaching her to rebuild her body and her life. She was emotional, unhappy, and very tearful, but somehow those months passed by, and she was eventually discharged.

Alas, the poor girl did not realise that life was now going to be tougher than ever. The flat she lived in and adored no longer seemed the same; she had great difficulty in settling down again. She told us she felt as if she was closed in, and she kept saying that it was like being in a deep hole. The doctors advised us that the only way for her to regain her confidence and strength was for us to let her get used to her own way of life. She tried to escape to my mum's to spend the nights there for comfort. It was almost more than we could bear to see her in this state—she had always been so brave. Naffilla would go long periods without visiting my house. Then, all of a sudden, through her fear of being alone in her flat, she would phone me and ask me to pick her up. I felt distraught because she had always been so kind to me, and my children. I did not want to disappoint her by saying no, so I did fetch her a couple of times—but I always made sure that she was back in her flat later that same day. As I bring this book to a close, in the last few weeks it seems Naffilla has seen a ray of light, and she is beginning to cope in her flat by herself once more, taking care of herself. Inevitably, there are some good days and bad days. In fairness to her, she really is trying her best.

It is no exaggeration to say that Naffilla's illness has taken everything away from her—her thinking, her whole way of life. The nature of t' illness is such that both its victims and the family around them er untold suffering on so many levels. In Naffilla's case, we are f that we are a very close family, as we always have been, and we have long since learnt to support each other. At the back of our minds, though, we will always live with the fear of losing her. We just want our dear Naffilla to be able to cope, so that she is here to see our children and their children for a very long time to come.

Beautiful Naffilla Karsan.

CHAPTER 22

...And Not Forgetting the Govanis

Some members of my husband Amir Govani's family were early Ugandan Asian settlers in the UK well before the historic events of 1972—as early as the 1960s, in fact.

Grandmother Fatima was widowed when she was in her mid thirties, and she was left to run the household with her three sons (my father-in-law, Pyarali, and brothers Sherali and Akbar) And four daughters (Dolat. Seru, Sakar, and Sultan). Jetha Bapa, our grandfather, passed away, and so Bapa, my father-in-law, was the eldest and was pushed to be the bread earner. He opened up a small shop with his mother in Kononi, a little town near Kampala. Both worked very hard, and as time went on this paid off, with the family consequently investing into coffee factories, including a huge complex in Luwero. The highly successful business became very well-known as Jetha Visram Brothers.

By this time all the brothers were married and they lived together at Madras Gardens in Kampala with their siblings. My mother-in-law had eight children—four boys, Nurdin, Amir, Amin, and Samsu, and four girls, Dilshad, Naseem, Nilufa, and Parvis. Uncle Sherali had five children: Azad, Laila, Dilshad, Salim, and Karim. Uncle Akbar had one son, Amin.

In England, my father-in-law and brothers first bought hotels in Kensington and then a shop in Twickenham in the borough of Richmond. The family ran a beautiful convenience store and post office, with residential accommodation above. As the siblings got older, each family moved out to another address, as it was it was only fair that they should have their own roof over their heads.

But tragedy was in store for Uncle Sherali as his dear wife, Aunty Dollu, was diagnosed with liver cancer. In those days, treatment and the potential for cure were still very much in their infancy. With a sad inevitability, this beautiful young woman who had been so full of life passed away, leaving young children behind; Karim, the youngest, was only five. Uncle Sherali was devastated, but had to be strong for the rest of his family. He remarried Aunt Dollat. They both ran a post office and stores in Hampton for many years, and they have since settled in Longbuckby, a peaceful little town in Northamptonshire.

Azad is married to Gulnar and has three lovely girls, Aliya, Alisha, and Abida. In fact Gulnar was heavily pregnant with Alisha, and her contractions started on my wedding day, so they had to rushed into hospital, and Alisha was born. Alisha has recently gotten married to a young fine man, Imtiaz, and they are living up North. Salim is married to a very dear friend of mine, Anita, and they have two gorgeous girls, Sharleez and Inara. Anisha, her sisters, my sisters, and I grew up together. We got on so well, and Anisha's mum treated us like her daughters. Salim I knew from before I got married, because he too was a dear friend. Karim, the youngest brother, is married to Yasmin, and they have two lovely boys. Leila is married to Anu, and they have two lovely girls. Dilshad is living near Dad in Longbuckby, taking care of them. Amin, Uncle Akbar's son, is married to Zaheera with two lovely boys and a gorgeous daughter.

Bapa and the boys ran the shop in Twickenham from 8.00 a.m. to 10.00 p.m., seven days a week. The family was very charming and the customers adored them. The post office was always very busy, and almost the whole family was trained to run it. Dilshad, the eldest daughter, was married to Mohammad in Uganda, and they are now living in Canada with their lovely girls and boy, Natasha, Fiona, and Zavar. We attended Natasha's and Geoff's wedding in a gorgeous ceremony, a mixture of two cultures.

Nurdin, my eldest brother-in-law, got married to Laila. At first they were living in England, but they are now living in Canada with their lovely girls, Ayesha, Tysin, and Farah. Farah has just got engaged to a nice young man in a lovely Asian ceremony. Nurdin had excellent skills for building; in fact his house in Basingstoke was amazing, all designed by Laila and himself. Ayesha was only two when I got married, and it was a pleasure to have a baby around; she was adorable and a pleasant little one.

Nilufa is married to Shamsher, and they live in Milton Keynes. They also run a post office in a very peaceful area of Milton Keynes. They are a few doors away from Bapa and Mum, and they play a huge part in looking after them and conduct it extremely well with lots of love. It is really funny because Amir had borrowed Shamsher's car to impress me in my first date. As he was bringing me back, he decided to stop at Twickenham to point out his shop. Much to his surprise, his brother-in-law Shamsher was waiting at the shop for the car to be returned. Amir's secret was found out by me, because Shamsher had not realised that Amir had told me a lie about the car.

Their lovely girls and boy, Nimet, Aman, Anoushka, and Simeen, are all living in London and have done very well. Aman works for an investment bank, Simeen is an event manager, Anoushka and Nimet are both teachers. Nimet is married to Asif, a doctor, and they have two lovely children, Kayal and Zian.

Naseem is married to Mervin and is living in Osterly, London. Naseem used to work for Air France and was forever paying for the family's air tickets. She also took Farzana to Canada with her on many occasions, when Farzana was a child. Farzana would take a little briefcase with her colouring pencils and books, and she would draw pictures and occupy herself.

Through Naseem I met this lovely Indian actress, Anju Mahendra, and her mother, Shantiji, a true gem of whom I am very fond of. Shantiji always visits me when she's in London. Amir and I have visited her when we are in Mumbai. In fact, there is a Bollywood actor whom we were very fond of and who was an absolute superstar in the 1970s, and I always wanted to meet him. Whilst I was in Mumbai, Anju arranged an appointment to meet him, so Amir, Farzana (who was only six then), and I went. What a meeting this was—Rajesh Khanna was an incredible human being. There he was, in front of me and so down to earth. Farzana had a temperature, so Rajesh Khanna called out a doctor to see her. I felt like I was dreaming, but it was real, thank God. Unfortunately whilst writing this book I am sad to say that Rajesh Khanna is no longer with us. He passed away a few weeks back. I think the whole of the Indian Film Industry and his fans are really going to miss him. What a legend he truly was. We also met Jackie Shroff, another fine human being and a great actor.

Mervin and Naseem moved to Uganda for a while, but Mervin's mother, Peggy, was suffering from cancer, so they had to move back to England. Peggy was truly a gem, such a wonderful person, and she smiled until the end. I had a great bond with her, but unfortunately we lost her through cancer.

Parvis is married to Anish, and they were living in England but have now moved to Vancouver, running one of the finest restaurants there. They have two gorgeous girls, Aniqa and Anoushka, both the sisters are at university.

Amin lives in Uganda but travels back and forth to Bristol, where his family now live. His young lady, Shian, and three lovely children, Niqa, Adam, and Amar, live in Bristol. They often visit Ascot, and we share great times together.

Samsu and his wife, Shelina, live in Bristol with their daughters, Shabrina is at university whilst Shenisa and Shahera are at school. It is strange again, because Shelina's grandparents lived next door to us in Masindi Port. When I was about seven, I always used to play with a ball on their veranda. Ladoo Masi, Shelina'a grandmother, would always ask me in for lunch, and her grandfather would give me sweets from the shop. They were both very kind. It's truly a small world.

After I married Amir in 1985, I moved to Twickenham with the family. I came from a big family and so did not have much of a problem settling into another one of similar size! As a bonus, I had already grown up knowing "the boys"—these were Amir's brothers from Ismaili Jamat Khanna. After prayers, we used to congregate or meet up for social occasions, either at Lillie Road Hotel in Fulham or Olympia, London. Over the years, I have built a great bond with the family, and I must say how kind every member of the family has been to me, especially whilst I was ill.

Amir and I honeymooned at Dianni Beach, Mombasa, Kenya. He had suggested Kenya because he was very fond of his cousins, Minaz, Jalalu, Ashraf, Mehboob, and Altaz. We had considered visiting Uganda during our honeymoon, but those thoughts were dashed when one night we were travelling with Amir's cousins from Nandi Hills to Kisumu, and I had the devil in me. I insisted on driving, but when we had travelled only twenty kilometres, I hit a pothole and caused a massive crash. Our car rolled down the hill several times, but we were so lucky and survived this nightmare experience. I was taken to Nairobi Agakhan Hospital because the door handle had hit my knee and pushed out the bone through the skin. At first, when I managed to extract myself from the wrecked car, I felt no pain because my thoughts were only for the other passengers, including Amir. Luckily they all escaped with minor injuries. Thank God for that, otherwise I would have never forgiven myself. Also, I felt guilty because I had written off a car that had belonged to Jafer Masa and Roshan Masi, Amir's uncle and aunt. They were both so good to me and told us not to worry about the car. Their concern was our well-being—what a lovely couple.

On arrival back in England, and with me by now well on the road to recovery, I resumed my work with Midland Bank for about nine months and then decided to join the family business. I had made an amazing friend at the bank by the name of Beverly, who was like a sister to me. We lived in the same part of London, so we travelled to work together. Good friendships, they say, are made in heaven, and that's certainly how it seemed to me. We initially got to know each other after she had been walking past my dad's shop in Balham, London. She saw him and asked if he had a daughter who worked for Midland Bank, to which he replied yes. He asked her how she had known; she laughed and explained that it was "the big eyes". Dad and I had similar eyes. Was there no escape anywhere in the world? I just laughed when she introduced me to herself and told me about Dad. It was so funny. She came home on many subsequent occasions with her other half, Michael, and we shared a great friendship. What a superb human being.

Beverly was very upset to see me leave the bank, but it was the right choice, and we stayed great friends. I enjoyed working in the family shop, too, because I already had experience in occasionally helping Dad in his shop. I would go to the Ealing based Ismaili Jamat Khanna with Bapa and Maa. I used to enjoy going at dawn for prayers with Bapa; it was such a peaceful time of the morning, with no traffic on the roads.

This also helped me form a bonding with Bapa, my father-in-law, which in my heart I believe exists even today. We can talk and connect a lot about Uganda and the past. My father and Bapa grew up in Uganda knowing the same people, so we have a lot in common. My mother had always taught me to cook, but at home, due to my own lack of interest, I had failed to learn much except the basics. My mother-in-law set about correcting that gap in my knowledge and expertise.

Grandma Fatima was very strong for most of life, but she ended up with severe diabetes and hence had loss of memory. She had worked so hard to bring up the children. After a short illness, she died.

Life is a Lesson

Around 1990 some of the family decided to move to Hamilton, Ontario, Canada. There they lived for many years before some members eventually decided to return to England. I had Farzana in 1988, my first child, and we thought it was only fair that, with an extended family, we should now find our own feet. We made the move to Ascot and that late, late shop, followed by the move into property. This move signalled many changes for my life. It is a lovely part of the world, but Amir and I had to grow up very fast and take more responsibility. It was very strange at first because we were both used to living with a big family, but as time went on, the shop kept us so busy that we didn't have a minute to breathe.

Years have gone by and there is a lot of love and care amongst our family. I am sad to say the last year Bapa's health had deteriorated although he is much better now. As we have all experienced with age comes forgetfulness. Both Bapa and Maa have worked extremely hard over the years and faced many challenges of bringing up the children.

For Bapa, one cannot even imagine how hard it must have been for him at such a young age to harbor responsibility of such a huge family after the death of his father, Jetha Bapa. However, with hard work, help from his mother, Fatima Maa and family members managed to establish themselves as 'Jetha Visram and Sons' which with the help of the Almighty was a huge name in Uganda. Bapa and the family too, have always had great faith in God which guided them through. The family travel a lot to Uganda, a country which will always be embedded in their hearts too.

Mr and Mrs Pyarali and Dolat Jetha Govani
[MAA AND BAPA]

Master Kayal and Master Zian Hirani

Master Adam, Miss Niqa, Master Amar Govani
Half English, Half Indian.

Chapter 23

Life Is a Lesson

Since my expulsion and after spending so much time in England, although it has taken many years to get to a grip with life, I have come to realise how we are protected from the ultimate. The belief in God and His grace really pulled us through. I believe that forgiveness is a virtue and that two wrongs do not make a right. Being brought up in that sense gave us the strength to forgive and move on with life. Life is nothing but a lesson learnt. I am certain that pain and happiness comes into everyone's life, but how you take life is entirely up to you. Only God knows the bigger picture.

If we had held on to the past, we would not have moved on. One has to shed any resentment from the soul and set it free to move on. At the end of the day, we only lost our possessions, but our lives were intact, so with the grace of God we were the fortunate ones. Yet, there were many unfortunate people who lost lives in horrific ways. The entire expulsion is behind us now. As I look at people around the world and their suffering, I realise we were the lucky ones.

I feel as though I have accomplished this mission of telling the world about what really happened to us, but it taught us all a lesson about life and how to cope with it when faced with utmost difficulties, which thousands of people are still faced with today in the world. Don't allow the pain to drag through from generation to generation; move on. When one door closes, another always opens, so never give up hope. In our case, forgiveness came very easy because the majority of the Ugandan people were, and are, incredibly graceful. It was only the minority who teamed up with Amin's government and got power hungry. The normal Ugandan people were left with a lot of pain and suffering, which left marks on their bodies and hearts.

What about human behaviour? Unless you are grounded and have the fear of God in your heart, power can go to your head and change you overnight. I always teach my children to be humble and respect everyone. I want to pass onto them this story of mine of how to come out of a deep hole in life with it and face it, because this is life, and there will be situations that they will be faced with in their daily lives. They should always A thank God for being alive, and they should face it like true troopers.

My children have grown up in England amongst a very multicultural society, for which I am very grateful. They have been to Uganda on a holiday, thoroughly enjoyed the trip, and learnt a lot. England is home to them, where they have grown up, but there is no harm to tell them about my roots so that they have full knowledge of what happened. What I admire about them most is that they have learnt to accept people from all religions, colours and walks of life. They take people for what they are.

I have decided to remain in England, which gave me a safe haven alongside my families, on both sides, and my friends. Uganda and its lovely people will always remain embedded in my heart, but England is where my children were born, and it gave us a new beginning. Life faces a lot of challenges and obstacles, but every day is a new day with new challenges.

I would also like to point out that whilst I visited Uganda and my hometown of Masindi, I spoke to the headmaster Mr Businge and the governors of Masindi Public School, which I attended before the expulsion. I promised to help with school funding. These children are in need of school uniform, shoes, books, and more, which we in the West take for granted. A percentage of the profits from this book will go towards those lovely children whose faces are deeply embedded in my heartheart.

Chapter 24

Review and Reflections

If my return to Uganda after forty years was the realisation of a lifetime's ambition, there is something else that is not far behind in that respect: this book. So far as I am concerned, this book simply had to be written—not just to tell the basic story about Idi Amin and the horrible aftermath of his wicked deed, but also to cover all those subsequent years when so many lives were totally rebuilt. I also wanted to sketch my story in the deeper historical background to it all, so that such important and valuable knowledge would not be lost to future generations.

Alas, the project has taken on an identity all of its own. I confess that there have been times when my enthusiasm for it has all but got the better of me. It has become something of an all-consuming passion, and I have little doubt that occasionally those closest to me may have privately questioned my wisdom (and sanity) in tackling such a big challenge.

I also confess that I may have fallen into the trap of too much information, but whenever in doubt, I have always taken the view that the information should go in, rather than be left out. I am also aware that, to you, dear reader, the narrative may appear to have wandered somewhat. In conclusion, therefore, I am writing this closing chapter in an attempt to piece together a summary of the events that I have covered, to remind the reader what the book has been about, along with some final reflections on what it has all meant. Please indulge me one last time, and then move on. But please, never forget this story.

Idi Amin was a military leader and the president of Uganda from 1971 to 1979. He had joined the British colonial regiment the King's Rifles in 1946. He rose to the rank of Major General and became the regiment's commander before seizing power in the historic military coup in 1971. Amin was a very cruel man who abused human rights and practised corruption on a vast scale. He encouraged extra-judicial killings and had around half a million Ugandans murdered during his rule. These killings were motivated by ethnic, political, and financial factors.

On August 4, 1972, Amin declared that he had a dream in which God told him the Asians in his country were no good for its economy and should be expelled. He began with expulsion of the British Ugandan Asians and announced that he would have talks with the UK high commissioner in Uganda, Richard Slater, to arrange for the repatriation of Asian British passport holders to leave Uganda, and he gave them three months to do this.

Three days later, on August 7, Amin announced that all non-Ugandan Asians should leave in three months' time. The neighbouring countries, such as Kenya, closed their borders to keep out the expelled Asians.

On August 11, Lady Tweedsmuir Belhelvie, who was the minister of foreign and commonwealth affairs in Britain, insisted that Mr Geoffrey Rippon, a prominent member of Edward Heath's Conservative government, should visit Uganda and other East African countries in a bid to persuade Amin to change his mind. Mr Rippon was invited by Idi Amin to Uganda to discuss the issue, but Amin did not change his mind. Rather, he told the press, "I see no more future for the Asians and will be very, very happy if they go." He said the British should take their responsibility, and England should accept those who were British passport holders. He also reiterated that the ninety-day deadline remained.

On August 16, the airlift out of Uganda for the British passport holders began. However, at the other end in Britain, there were right-wing marches taking place with the message that there was no need for further permanent immigration. Sir Edward attracted much criticism in this. At the same time, the president of the National Union of Students and the president of the Makerere University, Uganda's largest and second-oldest institution of learning, held talks with Amin to counter the opposition to his stance.

Amin took control of the airlines in Uganda and also stated that non-citizens could only fly with East African Airways. He seized all Asians' assets and made clear that not a shilling was to be taken out of Uganda without prior notice and permission. The UK, meanwhile, asked fifty countries to re-settle some of the Asians, and Joseph Godber, Minister of State for Foreign and Commonwealth Affairs, flew to Geneva for talks with Prince Sadrudin Agakhan, who was at that time the United Nations High Commissioner for Refugees. He then met with Dr Kurt Waldeim, the UN Secretary General.

Amin was a madman who fabricated stories and accused Britain of plotting against him to have him assassinated. He was so furious that on September 13, he announced plans to put Asians who were still in Uganda into concentration camps. On September 18, the first lot of Asians arrived in Britain, landing at Stansted Airport. These were 193 passengers flying on the old BOAC (British Overseas Airways Corporation). Half of these re-housed themselves with relatives, and the others were camped at Stradishall, a village in Suffolk.

Then, on September 22, eight thousand more were given forty-eight hours to leave or face the death penalty. Amongst these were my Grandma Baa, my Aunt Laila, and my twin uncles Hassan and Hussein. They got out as soon as they could because of the fear of being tortured. In Britain there was discussion on how to re-house the Asians, and as a result transit camps were set up.

In October of that year, Amin expelled Richard Slater, the high commissioner to Britain, accusing him of issuing propaganda against Uganda. Then he ordered all the professors to leave Uganda. His final deadline for the expulsion of all the Asians was November 8. He wanted reports on all those that were left behind, which were less than a thousand. These were Ugandan nationals or expatriates from countries other than the United Kingdom. Amongst these was my father, Uncle Hadi, and Uncle Sherali and his wife, Aunt Rashida.

My mother and the rest of the family were lucky to get out and go to Britain because they had British passports, but the fate of my father and his brothers lay in the hands of God. We are so grateful to Prince Sadrudin Agakhan for his role in negotiating a deal that secured the transfer of those who were left behind to other European countries, and hence into safe haven; otherwise the consequences would have been unimaginable.

After the expulsion of the Asians, Amin broke off diplomatic ties with Britain and nationalised eighty-five British-owned businesses. In 1973 US ambassador Thomas Melady reduced his presence in Uganda because of the brutal and unpredictable regime. Finally, for safety's sake, its embassy in Kampala was closed.

In 1976, Amin, with his corrupt ways, allowed an Air France airliner, which had been hijacked by ten members of the Popular Front for the Liberation of Palestine and two members of the German Revolutionaire Zellen, to land at Entebbe Airport. Those passengers who did not hold Jewish passports were flown to safety, but the others were held hostage. A group of Israeli commandoes seized control of the airport, freeing the hostages in a daring mission that spawned two movies. Three hostages died and ten were wounded; seven hijackers were killed. A seventy-five-year-old woman, Dora Bloch, was taken to Mulago Hospital in Kampala before the rescue operation and was then murdered in reprisal. This further soured Uganda's international relations.

As the years went by, Amin's erratic behaviour only worsened. The Ugandan infrastructure collapsed, and his popularity declined as people lost faith in the government. During 1977-1979, Uganda was reported to UNO on human rights. Dissent within Uganda and Amin's attempt to annex the Kagera province from Tanzania led to a war that resulted in Amin fleeing into exile in Libya, and then in Saudi Arabia. It was in Saudi Arabia that he passed away on August 16, 2003, thus bringing to a close one of the darkest chapters in the history of mankind.

In closing, therefore, I would like to articulate a few more reflections. It took many years to come to terms with all that had happened, and to adjust to our new life in England, but in the process I gradually came to realise how we are protected from the ultimate. More than anything, the belief in God and His grace was what really pulled us through. I believe that forgiveness is a virtue and that two wrongs do not make a right. Being brought up to believe such things has provided the strength to forgive and move on with life. Life is nothing but a lesson learnt. Pain and happiness enter the life of everyone, but how you take life is entirely up to you.

I hope I have succeeded in my mission to tell the world about what really happened to us. As much as anything else, our experiences taught us all a lesson about life and how to cope with it when faced with the utmost adversity. Pain should not be allowed to drag on from generation to generation; we have to move on. When one door closes, another always opens. One should never give up hope—never.

In our case, forgiveness came very easily because the majority of the Ugandan people were and are incredibly grateful. Today President Musevini has been fabulous in inviting the Asians back to Uganda, and if it that had not been the case, many others like me would have not been able to go back.

Also from the depths of my heart, I cannot conclude without thanking all those people who have been incredibly helpful and supportive to us in ensuring our survival and making possible our subsequent journey though life. Without their kindness, faith, and loving prayers, so much would not have been possible, and I thank in particular:

The British Government
- His Highness Prince Sadruddin Agakhan
- Sir Edward Heath
- Lord Robert Carr
- Prime Minister Pierre Trudeau
- President Yoveri Musevini
- Kurt Waldheim
- Volunteers in the camps
- Hassan Karsan

At the same time we must never forget those who were not so lucky. In closing, therefore, I extend my deepest condolences to the families of those Asians and local Ugandans who lost their lives at the hands of Idi Amin and his henchmen

I would like to point out that a certain amount of the profit from the sales of this book is going towards the re-building of Masindi Public School. When I visited Uganda last year the faces of those innocent children that I met at the school are embedded deeply in my heart.

Lightning Source UK Ltd.
Milton Keynes UK
UKOW041341021112

201604UK00002B/1/P